AMAR A

SIDHARTH BHATIA has been a journalist for over thirty-five years, working both in India and abroad. He is a regular commentator in newspapers and on television on current affairs, society and culture. He was awarded the press fellowship to Wolfson College in Cambridge University in 1990 and made an associate fellow of the college in 2001. A foreign correspondent in South Africa during the transition to democracy in 1993–94, he moved to Mauritius in 2003 to start a media company. He was in the editorial board that launched *DNA* in Mumbai in 2005 and ran the editorial page of the paper till the end of 2009. He is passionate about old cinema, Indian and Western, and about Mumbai, where he lives with his wife and two daughters. He is the author of *Cinema Modern: The Navketan Story* (2011), published by HarperCollins India.

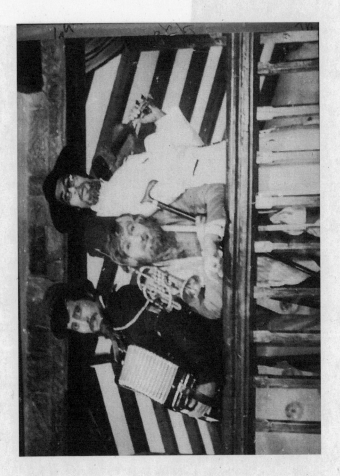

Amar Akbar Anthony

Masala, Madness and
Manmohan Desai

Sidharth Bhatia

HarperCollins *Publishers* India

First published in India by
HarperCollins *Publishers* in 2013
A-75, Sector 57, Noida, Uttar Pradesh 201301, India
www.harpercollins.co.in

4 6 8 10 9 7 5 3

P-ISBN: 978-81-7223-935-0
E-ISBN: 978-93-5029-985-2

Typeset in 11/15 Adobe Garamond at
SŪRYA

Printed and bound at
Replika Press Pvt. Ltd.

To
Almona, Aliya and Rhea

Contents

1

Heart of Madness

'You see the whole country of the system is juxtapositioned by the haemoglobin in the atmosphere because you are a sophisticated rhetorician intoxicated by the exuberance of your own verbosity.'

These are hardly words that would sit well in a poem, and even less in a Hindi film song. And yet, this bit of whimsy kicks off one of the most exuberant songs of the 1970s, a madcap romp during which the hero (Amitabh Bachchan) woos his sweetheart (Parveen Babi) right from under the nose of her well-muscled escort during an Easter dance.

Somewhat like jabberwocky, these nonsensical words do not mean anything, but fit in well with the mood of the moment and also with the on-screen character of Anthony Gonsalves, a frivolous young street-smart 'tapori' who is a bootlegger by profession and a tough guy by inclination. But he is a romantic and has the proverbial golden heart. How can anyone not like him?

Anthony has been waiting for 'The One' and from the moment he sees the girl walk into the church one day, he is in love. In his words, 'Violins played in my head, a bell rang in my heart.' But he does not know how to get close to her since she is always accompanied by her tough-looking bodyguard Zebesco. He invites her for a date but learns she is already committed to attending an Easter dance, an important date on the social calendar of young Christian boys and girls in Bombay. That gives Anthony an idea—he lands up there, wearing a top hat, coat-tails and a monocle: quite the gent. Making a dramatic entrance by stepping out of a giant Easter egg, he sings and dances for her, baring his heart for her to see.

'*My name is Anthony Gonsalves,*' he declares.

The song, with a crazy jumble of English words juxtaposed between the verses, was written by Anand Bakshi. What is less known is that the nonsensical sentences were the work of Amitabh Bachchan. He used to mumble all kinds of gibberish—random English words strung together that did not particularly make sense but sounded impressive—all the time. 'It was a habit from college. The words didn't mean anything at all,' he says. Manmohan Desai had heard Bachchan mutter the bit about the 'sophisticated rhetorician intoxicated ... verbosity' (which is an almost exact quote by British politician Benjamin Disraeli in 1878, except that Disraeli had used the term *inebriated* instead of *intoxicated*). Amused by its sheer absurdity, Desai asked Bachchan about it. 'But there was nothing to tell, it was just plain old nonsense.' Desai saw potential in this nonsense and slowly the idea was born to include the words in the song. Bachchan sang the lines himself.

Despite this collaborative effort, much of the credit for the sequence should go to Desai. As the master of the masala film, he had a sharp eye and ear for what would work. He even worked closely with dance director Kamal for the steps and came up with the idea of dressing Bachchan in a top hat, tails and a monocle. The pièce de résistance was the large Easter egg out of which the character of Anthony emerges.

In all his films, Desai demonstrated remarkable felicity for telling a good story in an entertaining way, with all the key ingredients of a good Hindi commercial film—comedy, pathos, drama, high emotion—mixed with a few catchy tunes, lavish sets and good-looking stars for the perfect confection. What distinguished him from others was his light touch—he knew when to pull back.

In *Amar Akbar Anthony*, his first film as a producer, he got the recipe just right. Not one scene or moment is out of place. The whole package comes together perfectly and the film's great strength is the fact that four decades on, it still has the ability to engage the next-generation viewer.

Amar Akbar Anthony was Desai's fourteenth film (IMDB shows thirteen films before this one). He was barely forty years old when he began directing it and it was finished in less than a year. Desai, who had made not even a film a year since his debut in 1960 with *Chhalia*, had suddenly turned prolific; in 1976, he was directing no less than four films at the same time: *Dharam Veer*, *Chacha Bhatija*, *Parvarish* and *Amar Akbar Anthony*. All of them were released in 1977 and each one went on to become a super hit. This was at a time when movies played in large single-screen cinemas, often with a seating capacity of nearly a thousand, and were considered a big success only if they ran for at least twenty-five continuous weeks, the much-coveted silver jubilee. These days, films have to score big only in the opening weekend, and that too in small, multiplex theatres.

Both *Amar Akbar Anthony* and *Dharam Veer* hit the seventy-five-week-run mark, propelling Desai to the very top as the most successful director of the year and arguably of that decade. The energetic, excitable and entertaining Desai turned into a superstar himself—he was the man with the golden touch, the man who knew how to propitiate the elusive box-office goddess. His peers wondered what his strength was—they too used the same stars, engaged the same music directors and had infused their own films with the same spicy concoctions that he did, and yet no one else had his strike rate. What was the secret 'X' ingredient Manmohan Desai used?

His earlier films in the decade like *Rampur Ka Lakshman*, *Sachaa Jhutha* and *Roti* had also been hits but nothing as big as what he achieved in 1977, most notably with *Amar Akbar Anthony*. This film became his crowning glory and none of his films after that—most of them successful—brought him the fame and the respect this one did. With *Amar Akbar Anthony*, this simple man from a simple neighbourhood of Mumbai, who prided himself as being in touch with the Everyman, became the most sought-after commodity in the fickle world of the Indian film industry. It was, in many ways, a sweet vindication for him.

Manmohan Desai was born in a family of film-makers in Mumbai on 26 February 1937. The Indian film industry was in its infancy at the time, with Mumbai being just one of the centres of production, along with Kolkata, Pune, Lahore and some cities in the south of India. Desai's father, Kikubhai Desai, was the owner of Paramount Studios which made over fifty films during the silent era. These were mainly mythologicals though nothing survives of them.

Ketan, Manmohan Desai's son, says his

grandfather's company was sued by Paramount of Hollywood for copyright infringement. Instead of balking and backing down, Kikubhai engaged the best-known lawyer of the day, Muhammad Ali Jinnah, and despatched him to London to fight the case. 'We won,' Ketan says with some satisfaction.

But when Kikubhai died suddenly at the young age of thirty-nine, the family's fortunes took a nosedive. The widow had to settle all the debts and she sold everything she had, except the studio, which eventually became Filmalaya.

From living in a sprawling bungalow in Versova, the family moved to a cramped chawl in Khetwadi in south Mumbai. Khetwadi is an old neighbourhood where century-old buildings stand cheek-by-jowl, propping each other up. The neighbourhood is predominantly a Gujarati one though there are several Maharashtrian chawls too. It is part of old Mumbai, not too far from the grungy red-light areas, where Desai's dialogue writer Kader Khan was growing up.

In Khetwadi's Pratap Niwas, in a small flat, young Manmohan lived with his siblings, including elder brother Subhash who worked with Homi

Wadia. Subhash Desai then entered the family business as an independent producer, making films like *Circus Queen*, *Golden Gang*, *Aati Nag Kanya* and *Shaikh Chilli*. His biggest film was a mythological, *Samrat Chandragupt* (1958), on which Manmohan was an assistant.

One of the elder Desai's associates was the great Babubhai Mistry, the earliest pioneer of special effects. Mistry was the acknowledged master of magic tricks on the screen for producers like the Wadia brothers. He used to turn heroes into parrots and women into snakes on the screen, all valuable skills in mythological and fantasy films. Young Manmohan, who was uninterested in studying (he said later he was asked by his college to leave), joined Mistry as an apprentice and worked in that capacity for two years. (Though he never acquired the craft of producing special effects, in his later years, Manmohan put those ideas to great use in his films.)

In 1959 or thereabouts, Subhash Desai decided to produce a film and asked his younger brother to direct it. 'My father laid down one condition,' remembers Ketan. 'He said he wanted his favourite star and the biggest name of the day, Raj Kapoor, to act in the film.' This was a tall order but Subhash nonetheless took Manmohan to Raj Kapoor and said, 'Raj, he wants to direct you.' The star was sceptical. 'But he is barely twenty-one.' My uncle told him, 'Raj, when you made *Barsaat*, you were just twenty-four. What if the other actors had said no to you?'

Kapoor told the young hopeful that he would act in one shooting schedule to gauge whether the director had it in him. If he did not like the final results, he would walk out. 'My uncle told Raj Kapoor, "You are free to walk out, but I will keep the director."' Manmohan shot the song '*Dum dum diga diga*' and when he showed Raj Kapoor the rushes, the star predicted the young man would go far and become a famous director one day.

Despite its popular songs, its big stars and its somewhat unusual theme—the heroine is a married woman—*Chhalia* was only moderately successful at the box office. In a later interview, Desai said it ran up against *Mughal-e-Azam*, the big blockbuster of the era. A day would come when Desai would be the bigger fish in the water and other film-makers would worry about releasing films opposite his.

Subhash Desai decided to make his next film, *Bluff Master*, with Shammi Kapoor, then a rising young star with hits like *Tumsa Nahin Dekha*, *Junglee* and *Professor* behind him. Halfway through the filming, *Bluff Master* ran into financial problems and Manmohan Desai had to release an almost unfinished version to placate the financiers and distributors who wanted to recover their investment. The film is largely unmemorable except for the song '*Govinda ala re*', which became a huge hit. It was shot in Khetwadi, outside the chawl where the director lived, and brilliantly captures the exuberant energy of public festivals in the city. It is tempting to see the early stirrings of '*Tareef teri nikli hai dil se*', the qawwali in *Amar Akbar Anthony*, in this song; both show public devotion to a popular deity. At his best, Desai was a master at sensing the pulse of the man on the street.

Bluff Master flopped miserably and the Desai brothers went into hibernation, becoming untouchables in an industry that only respects success. 'A producer would ring me up and say he was coming, and then he wouldn't show up. So two years went past without any work,' Manmohan Desai later told an interviewer, Connie Haham.

Shammi Kapoor, who was to later become a good friend and relative—their children eventually married—asked him to finish a half-done film, *Budtameez*, on a fee of Rs 500 a day. The film was poorly made, so Desai remade it from scratch. *Budtameez* was one of those typical Shammi Kapoor films capitalizing on his wild and fun image and did reasonably well, but still, work was slow in coming.

Budtameez was followed two years later by *Kismat*, an action film with Biswajeet and Babita (remembered for its peppy songs, including the chart-busting '*Kajra mohabbatwala*' which had Biswajeet doing a memorable turn in drag) and then, again after a two-year gap, in 1970, came *Sachaa Jhutha*, with the biggest star of the time, Rajesh Khanna. Desai wrote the script himself. The film, with Khanna in a double role, was a bona fide commercial success and had many of Manmohan Desai's special touches—a handicapped character, peppy songs and twists and turns in the plot, culminating with a court scene in which the crucial evidence is provided by a dog.

Animals, birds, snakes, they all have found a

place in Desai's films. In *Bhai Ho To Aisa*, he used a cobra; in *Coolie*, Bachchan had a falcon (an Islamic touch, that), and in *Mard* it was a horse who perfectly understood his master. Similarly, characters in many of his films were handicapped and often blind (*Roti*, *Amar Akbar Anthony*). In *Aa Gale Lag Jaa*, the polio-stricken boy no doubt added to the emotional element of the story, always a handy device to pull in the female audiences. Desai has been quoted as saying that his heart went out to handicapped people, and especially to those who were blind.

In *Amar Akbar Anthony*, Nirupa Roy's loss of sight allowed Desai to weave in several plot twists; she keeps running into her sons but cannot recognize them. It is a moot point why they don't recognize her, since the eldest at least was a big boy when the family broke up.

It wouldn't do to end the film with the mother still blind, so Desai makes sure her eyesight is restored after her youngest son Akbar sings a qawwali to Shirdi Saibaba, a revered mystic who lived in western India in the early part of the twentieth century. He has millions of followers among Hindus as well as Muslims. The song was a relatively late addition to the film and no doubt contributed to its box-office success. Desai was nothing if not canny about what would click. It was his boast that he knew the minds and hearts of the masses.

'My father was a very rooted man,' recalls Ketan Desai. 'He lived for most of his life in Pratap Niwas in Khetwadi and played cricket on the streets and in the maidans close by. Even after he had made many films, in the evenings he used to hang around with his local friends and chat with them. They used to praise or criticize his films, tell him where he had failed. His logic was simple: "These are my audience, my customers; I have to take them seriously." He was very grounded and that helped him stay connected with his audience. Without that rootedness he couldn't have delivered seventeen super hits out of the twenty films he made. The streets also gave him inspiration. This is where he found his characters and his stories.

'Many of his characters were created out of his own personal observations. Akbar was an amalgamation of the youngsters who lived in predominantly Muslim areas which he had seen and Anthony was inspired by a bootlegger who ran a still in the tiny four-feet gap between our building and the next,' says Ketan. Lending credibility to the street credentials of these on-screen characters were the lines penned by Kader Khan, himself a man who had grown up in the crowded and unsavoury neighbourhood of Kamathipura, better known as the red-light area of Mumbai.

'My father used to suddenly wake up at three in the morning with an idea or two. Ideas used to come to him all the time and then he was all enthusiastic, full of energy, wanting to pin it down. If he was convinced, that was it. Then whether the star or the trade pundits or the financiers found flaws in it, he would pursue it to the end.'

One such idea came to Desai while reading a newspaper story about a man who dropped his three sons in a park and then set out to commit suicide. The same evening, the writer Prayag Raaj came to the Desai household to borrow keys to the director's farmhouse. Desai mentioned the story to him and asked, 'What if the man did not commit suicide after all, returned to the park and found his three sons missing. How would he react?'

Raaj, who had worked with Desai in the past, took the idea further. 'What if the three boys were taken away by three people—one a Muslim, another a Christian and the third a Hindu?' That was the kernel which was fleshed out to come up with the story.

They kept on chatting animatedly till midnight. Raaj postponed his plans to go out of town and they met the next day to develop the story further. (Ketan Desai says his mother too chipped in with a few ideas, which is why she is credited in the film for 'story'.) Suddenly Raaj said, 'Manji, I will give you my part of the story only if you produce it. You have made people rich with your work. Time you worked for yourself.'

Ketan continues, 'My father was totally uninterested in money. He did not want to produce films but my mother pressed him to try it at least once.' Finally Desai agreed. And then he came up with the name—*Amar Akbar Anthony*. 'Just like that,' says Ketan, snapping his fingers.

For Amar, the understated police inspector, Desai chose Vinod Khanna. For Akbar, the street-smart Muslim boy, he selected Rishi Kapoor. Some of his advisers were not so sure. 'Rishi has an upper-class face, would it work as a qawwal, people asked him,' recalls Ketan. But Manmohan Desai was convinced and unshakeable. But it was his decision to take Bachchan, known then for his intense, serious persona, as the happy-go-lucky Anthony that surprised everyone. 'I have seen comic potential in him,' he claimed.

Once the idea began taking shape, Desai called up his stars. Most of them thought initially that they were being selected for a historical film, a la *Dharam Veer* which he was making at the time. 'Vinod Khanna thought he would play Amar Singh Rathod, Rishi Kapoor got the impression that he would play Akbar the Great, which his grandfather Prithviraj Kapoor had enacted so convincingly in *Mughal-e-Azam*, and Bachchan's first thought was that this was Mark Antony's role.'

Rishi Kapoor breaks into a chuckle as he recalls getting a phone call from Desai. 'I was in Bikaner shooting for *Laila Majnu*. I got a call from my secretary telling me that Manmohan Desai wanted to speak to me. Those were the days when there were no cellphones and you had to book a trunk call, or a lightning call. Sometimes the call used to materialize after four days or so. Plus you had to shout on the phone. Anyway, I was playing billiards with my co-stars after the shoot and the call came. I went to the hotel reception to take it. I heard him say: I want you to play Akbar. Now I had had a drink or two. I wondered what he was talking about. Akbar? My grandfather had played it. I told him that and he said no, I want to make a film called *Amar Akbar Anthony*. I thought it was one of his historical dramas, with Akbar and Mark Antony. You know MKD was capable of doing anything. He was shooting *Dharam Veer* at the time, a historical, Romanesque kind of film.

'I put the phone down and started abusing him; in Mumbai he was telling my secretary, "What kind of boss you have?" Now if you imagine that moment to be like a split screen—Manji in Mumbai abusing me to my secretary, me in Bikaner telling my friends he has lost it. Anyway, I came to Mumbai after three days, and met him and once I realized what he meant, I was apologetic.'

For Kapoor, it is a happy memory, since it led

to one of his best roles. He goes on: 'Funnily enough, when I was making *Bobby* with my father, Manmohan Desai was making *Rampur Ka Lakshman* with my brother Randhir. He told my brother, "Has your father gone mad? He has chosen a four-foot-tall hero." And he had also said something similar about Amitabh Bachchan, stating that this six-footer will go nowhere. I reminded him of that when he signed me; it was a kind of poetic justice.'

Bachchan, already working with Desai in *Parvarish*, remembers being told by Desai that he was launching his production banner with a new film, *Amar Akbar Anthony*, and wanted him to star in it. 'Are you mad,' I said. '*Amar Akbar Anthony* just sounded like a crazy title,' says Bachchan. 'He turned and said to me, "Lalla (he called me by that nickname), after the movie is released, whenever you walk down the street, people will call you Anthony."'

When he decided to make *Amar Akbar Anthony*, Desai was working on three other films simultaneously: *Parvarish*, *Dharam Veer* and *Chacha Bhatija*. The casts of these films overlapped—Dharmendra was in the latter two,

Neetu Singh was in the first two. Desai would go from set to set directing a scene or two for the day. (Sometimes a few characters overlapped too— Shabana Azmi played a pickpocket in *Parvarish* as well as in *Amar Akbar Anthony*.)

This also meant that Desai had several sets standing at any given time. 'Once, Raj Kapoor complained to his manager that he just couldn't get space in his own studio. He wanted to know who was using the sound stages. The manager told him they were all booked for Manmohan Desai films,' says Ketan. Desai used to sit in the centre of RK studios, at a kind of crossroads of all the four sound stages, and issue instructions to his assistants—put a trolley there, put some lights there, prepare for this scene in a third. It was all in his head, without paperwork, without notes. Then he used to walk in and shoot. 'He was a flipping genius,' says Ketan with fondness and awe.

Directors, at least in India, do not shoot in linear sequence. Shooting schedules depend on a lot of variables, not the least of them being the availability of the stars' 'dates', since the big names work on more than one film at any given time. They give their available dates weeks and months in advance and it is up to the film-maker to keep everything ready so that no time is wasted. Desai was a reasonably big director and by using the same star for more than one film he managed to lock them in, but even so, the shooting was done patchily. The songs and the 'items' were done first.

'Nowadays we hear a lot about putting in a couple of items (set pieces) in a film,' says Bachchan. 'Manji was the originator of that idea.' These items, whether or not relevant to the larger context of the story, provided entertainment and repeat value; audiences remembered them and came back again and again to see them. Three such set pieces in *Amar Akbar Anthony* were the Easter egg scene, the Saibaba qawwali and Bachchan's drunken scene in front of a mirror. Though all were well integrated into the story, they could easily have not existed without any loss to *Amar Akbar Anthony*. Indeed, they could have been lifted and inserted into another film and no one would have been wiser or have cared. It was as if the director and the scriptwriter had had Eureka moments when brainstorming about how best to perk up a scene, and the items were then inserted at critical points to keep the audience interested. Irrespective of how it happened, the fact is they worked and worked brilliantly. It is difficult to imagine *Amar Akbar Anthony* without two of Bachchan's best-known scenes.

Desai had no shortage of such 'out of the box', crazy ideas that clicked, which not only made him the Badshah of the box office but gave rise to a whole new genre of films named after him. Today, his name is a byword for the improbable yet somehow logical situation, as in 'this sounds like a Manmohan Desai film'. How many directors can boast of this?

2

Lost and Found: The Story

The gates of the central jail open and a man in white clothes steps out. This is Kishen Lal (Pran), a convict who has just served a jail sentence. He heads straight home to meet his family, which consists of a wife and three little sons. He has picked up toys for them. Just as he is about to reach his home, a neighbour informs him that his wife and family are in a bad way. His wife Bharti has been suffering from tuberculosis and his sons have not eaten for days.

In his modest cottage, he finds his wife Bharti (Nirupa Roy) coughing in the manner of a consumptive patient. His three boys are squabbling over a little bit of food. She touches his feet as good Indian wives do (at least in films). 'Didn't Robert send money regularly?' asks Kishen. 'No,' says his wife, 'and even if he had, I would have returned it. I do not want to feed my family with ill-gotten money.'

His two older sons meanwhile are fighting over a toy gun their father has brought for them. The eldest hides it in the ground near the house. The youngest, too young to speak, just cries.

An angry Kishen rushes to Robert's palatial home and confronts him. Kishen used to be Robert's driver. Robert had come to Kishen's house one day, pleading with him to take the rap for a driving accident in which a pedestrian was killed. Robert had promised Kishen he would take care of his family by sending them twice his salary but had reneged on the deal the moment Kishen went to jail. Kishen reminds him of that promise.

Robert feigns ignorance of any such commitment and mocks Kishen Lal, pouring whisky on his own shoes and asking the driver to clean them. Kishen feels humiliated but complies. Robert compounds the insult by tossing a coin to Kishen as his fee and asks his flunkeys to throw the driver out. Kishen warns Robert that he will take revenge, grabs a gun from one of the goons and fires at Robert, but the gangster is wearing a bulletproof jacket and laughs it off. Kishen then dives out through a window, gets into a car and escapes. The car holds a box full of smuggled gold (which Kishen is unaware of) and a panic-stricken Robert orders his men to get the loot back. (Gold was the item of choice for smugglers in the 1970s).

Kishen rushes home to pick up his family but finds his wife gone. She has left a letter informing him that she wants to commit suicide and that the family is now his responsibility. She has left behind a locket with a picture of their family deity, Santoshi Maa. He hurriedly puts the kids in his car and takes them to a park where he asks them to wait under a statue of Mahatma Gandhi while he goes and deals with Robert's men who are following him. Kishen's hurried departure from his home has been noticed by a neighbour who happens to be a police constable.

After the father drives off from the park, the eldest son runs after the car but is knocked unconscious by the goons' car. The second son goes off to find some food for his crying brother. The mother, who has set out to commit suicide, is hit by a falling tree and loses her eyesight. Kishen, driving fast to escape his followers, loses control and his car goes down a ravine where it bursts into flames. The bad guys are about to go into the ravine to retrieve the gold when a police party driving past orders that nobody should venture near the car. The constable who had seen Kishen leave recognizes the car and assumes that Kishen and the children have died in the crash.

The youngest child, who was crying alone in the park, is picked up by a kindly old Muslim praying in a mosque nearby. He feels Allah has sent him the child and decides to adopt it as his own. Driving back, he comes across an unconscious Bharti and offers to take her back to her home. It is raining heavily. She thanks him and asks about the crying child in the front seat. She cannot see and doesn't know it is her own son. He tells her he found him in a park. All this action takes just a little over ten minutes of screen time.

Kishen Lal comes to and sees that his car is a wreck. He picks up the box of gold and makes his way to the park where he had left his sons.

The second child has meanwhile returned to

the park with some food but finds no one there. He runs to a church to take shelter from the rain. He is found there the next morning by a kindly priest who takes him in. 'Come on, son, God will protect you,' says the priest.

When Bharti comes back home, she is told by the police constable that her husband and children have died. She is distraught and breaks her bangles against the door (a gesture symbolizing widowhood, often used in Hindi films).

The eldest son, who was knocked down by a car, is discovered by a police inspector who takes him home.

Kishen Lal, who is returning with the gold to the park where he had left the children, sees the police jeep and hides. After the jeep is gone, he rushes to the park, but the children are gone.

The scene now shifts to a confessional in a church. A little boy, neatly dressed in a school uniform, is confessing to a priest that he has sold all his schoolbooks. The priest chides him, upon which the child says that he sold the books to get some money to pay for the funeral of a man who died on the street. The priest is secretly pleased but tells the boy, 'You should have informed the police, my son.'

Cut to many years later, and the boy, now all grown up (Amitabh Bachchan), in the same confessional box, protests, 'No, father, I don't want to get involved with the police.' The priest reprimands Anthony, for that is his name, for being involved in illicit activities like manufacturing and selling liquor, whereupon the boy says proudly that not only is his business perfectly legal—he has a valid licence—but he also gives half his earnings to God (pointing towards Mother Mary with a baby Jesus) for charity.

While this banter is going on, someone comes running in and tells them that there has been an accident outside the church. Anthony rushes out and sees Bharti lying on the ground. He does not recognize her. She has been hit by a car. He calls for a cab and takes her to a hospital. Inspector Amar (Vinod Khanna), the eldest brother, is in his police station when he gets a call and he too proceeds to the hospital. In the very same hospital, Akbar (Rishi Kapoor), the baby of the Kishen Lal family, is flirting with a comely Dr Salma (Neetu Singh) by pretending to be sick. She scolds him for landing up again and again with the same excuse. This time, he says, he has come to invite her for a qawwali programme the same evening.

A nurse comes in and tells the doctor that an accident patient just brought in needs additional blood. Dr Salma asks Akbar to donate some blood, since it is of the same 'Rh' blood group. Sure, he says. Three men are lying on a bed and tubes from their arms are going into a common bottle to be transfused into Bharti. They are asked their names and they reply, one after the other, 'Amar', 'Akbar', 'Anthony', as the camera pans from one to the other. The titles begin, a full twenty-three minutes after the prelude (possibly the longest in Hindi films). In the background, a song plays, telling us that this is a true story. Blood is thicker than water, warbles the singer.

The scene cuts to Anthonywadi, a poor neighbourhood that is named after Anthony, who runs a bar there. It is clear that his writ runs here and this displeases the earlier boss of the area who has just returned from a stint in prison. The old-timer challenges the upstart and a fight breaks out. Anthony beats up the tough guy and disposes him off by throwing him in a garbage truck. It demonstrates not only his strength but also his flair for the dramatic.

Akbar, who seems to know Anthony, comes by

and gives an invitation card for the qawwali performance the same evening. 'Do you want me to help sell a few tickets?' asks Anthony. On the contrary, says Akbar, the show is sold out, and warns Anthony not to sell off the card in the black market. This is the second encounter among the two after they have grown up, the first being at the hospital. The family will continue meeting each other in all kinds of situations without being aware of their connection.

That evening, Akbar comes to the venue of the performance in style, in his foster-father's old vintage car and accompanied by his friends. A rapidly recovered Bharti has come to the hall too. She gives a bouquet of flowers to Akbar, wishing him success for the show. As he goes in, she begins to ask around for a ticket but none is available. She bumps into Anthony who says he has a special pass and can take her in. He allows her to sit on his seat, while sitting down next to her on the floor, a filial gesture that shows respect to a mother.

Inside the hall, Akbar sings with gusto, while all the time looking at his lady-love, Salma, who has come with her stern father Taiyyeb Ali who disapproves of her romance. She is in a burqa, but one that is diaphanous enough to show her face. The father refuses to let her lift the veil, but Akbar's singing charms her and at the end of the song she comes on the stage and hands him a rose. The crowd goes wild. Anthony joins in the fun, singing one line from the qawwali, a gesture no doubt included to please the cinema audiences.

In the police station, Inspector Amar is summoned by his boss and told about a con-girl who is running a scam on a quiet street. She thumbs a lift and once in the car, threatens them into parting with their belongings. A photographer has fallen victim but not before taking her picture. Amar's brief is to arrest the girl.

He goes to the spot in civilian clothes and sure enough, the girl waves down his car and seductively offers to take him to a secluded place where they can (presumably) romance. 'The police never comes to that place,' she says. If only she knew. Once they reach that spot, she tries to blackmail him, demanding he hand over his wallet or else she will shout for help. When he dares her to do so, she begins shouting and four unsavoury-looking men turn up. Inspector Amar reveals his identity and fights them off. However, while they run away, the girl stays put. She tells Amar that one of the men was her stepbrother and it is he who forced her into this sordid business. Amar asks the girl to move in with him. This is all very chaste, since the girl's grandmother also moves in, but after one appearance is never seen again.

We now hear again about Kishen Lal. He had used the gold he had found to build himself an empire in crime and smuggling. He bought off all of Robert's henchmen and had also kidnapped his baby daughter. Robert is now reduced to being just a small-time employee of Kishen Lal, carrying the smuggled goods that land on Bombay's coast.

When Robert pleads with Kishen to let him know where his daughter is, the latter behaves in exactly the same manner as Robert had all those years ago. He spills whisky on his shoes and asks Robert to clean it. Then he feigns a memory loss and tosses him the same coin. As Kishen turns to go, Robert grabs a gun and shoots Kishen in the back. Kishen is saved because he is wearing a bulletproof vest on his back, mirroring in reverse the scene between the two years ago. 'I knew you are a coward who would shoot a man when his back is turned,' says Kishen, bitingly.

The police reach the spot and Kishen escapes. Robert picks up a box of gold and shoots a police officer, who is the same man who had saved young Amar. Robert then runs away. While running he is deliberately tripped by Anthony who finds a gold biscuit that has fallen from the box. Anthony offers to help Robert but asks for one-third of the gold for himself and another third for God. Robert agrees.

Amar is angry that his foster-father has been shot. He tortures three of the men who were arrested in the police raid on the coast, asking them to name the man who fired at the cop. One of them says it was Robert. Amar wants to know whom they are working for. Before any of them can answer, Amar is called away. An eyewitness has been found who claims to have seen Robert with Anthony.

Amar lands up at Anthonywadi and confronts Anthony who behaves flippantly and tries to talk his way out. When Amar catches him by the collar, Anthony says no one has ever shown him such disrespect and had Amar not been in uniform he would have bashed him up. The scene is set for both of them to fight it out. Crowds collect to witness this epic clash and the music is of the spaghetti western variety. Amar takes off his shirt and gun, Anthony strikes an aggressive fighter's pose. The fight begins. Both try their moves, but it is clear that Amar has the upper hand and sure enough he wins. He is an inspector as well as the elder brother, after all. Anthony is hauled to the police station, bashed and bruised.

The next morning, Bharti comes to the police station to give flowers to Amar. She hears Anthony's voice and he tells her he has been jailed. She calls both of them 'beta' and vouches for Anthony. He says Amar is cold-hearted and will not melt by just words but points out to him that as 'Maaji' has called them both 'beta', they have become brothers. Amar is unimpressed by this sentimental argument. Bharti gives him a flower too.

Anthony is sent to the court in a Black Maria but on the way, the van runs into a smoke bomb and when the fog clears, Anthony is missing. He is kidnapped and taken to the palatial house of Kishen who wants to know where Robert is. Anthony offers his flower to Kishen and notices that Kishen is wearing a locket with Santoshi Maa on it. Seeing Anthony being frivolous and evasive, Kishen leaves, ordering his sidekicks to get the information, by violence if necessary.

Somehow Anthony escapes and voluntarily goes back to the police lock-up. Amar asks him why he has returned; Anthony says he did not want his 'brother' to lose his job. Amar tells him that Robert had shot a police officer. Anthony is shocked; he offers to take Amar to where Robert is hiding, but when they reach there, Robert has escaped again. Amar is angry with Anthony, holding him responsible.

A distraught Anthony is thinking about what to do next when the priest comes to see him and admonishes him, asking to give up his wayward ways. 'Get married,' suggests the priest, but Anthony says he is waiting for the right girl. When Ms Right comes on the scene, he will know, because 'violins will play in the background and bells will ring in my heart'.

The scene shifts to the airport where Kishen is waiting for Jenny to land. Jenny is Robert's daughter whom Kishen has brought up. He has even sent her abroad to study. Robert too is at the airport, disguised as a loader, to see whom Kishen receives. That way he figures he will know what his daughter now looks like.

Kishen is always a step ahead and says hello to a complete stranger (Helen). Robert kidnaps her and takes her away. Kishen then meets the real Jenny (Parveen Babi—her entrance comes an hour and ten minutes into the film). Kishen tells Jenny his story and how he ended up losing his three sons. This story makes a big impression on Jenny. At home, Kishen introduces her to Zebesco, who will from now on be her bodyguard and accompany her everywhere.

In the church one Sunday morning, Anthony is lighting all the lamps when he turns and sees a vision walking in. It is Jenny. True enough, the violins play and the bells ring in his heart. He is in love. After the service, he runs after her with a bag he says she has dropped. She says it is not her bag. Then he offers her a rose and asks her if she will come with him to the Easter dance that evening. She declines, saying she is going to the Catholic Gymkhana dance.

At the dance, a giant Easter egg is wheeled out and from there steps out a top-hatted, monocle-wearing gent in coat-tails and trousers. He sings

'*My Name is Anthony Gonsalves*', all the while trying to impress Jenny who is dancing with Zebesco. The latter gets furious and threatens to beat up Anthony who is too drunk to retaliate. Anthony heads home and staring at himself in the mirror berates himself for drinking and getting beaten up. So drunk is he that he applies medicine and Band-Aid to his image.

An upset Jenny goes to the church to confess to the priest that it was because of her that Anthony got a walloping. She confesses that she has fallen in love with him. Anthony is sitting in the priest's cubicle and hears everything. He is thrilled and is about to admit his own love for her, when she says they must leave the church. But there is a problem: Zebesco is waiting outside for her. Anthony whisks her away from another door and they run off to the seafront where they sing of their love for each other. The same emotion is expressed by the other two couples, Amar and Lakshmi, and Akbar and Salma. Each brother has found his true love.

Akbar calls out to Salma one evening, asking her to come down from her home because he wants to show her his new camera. She says she cannot, because her father is at home. Disappointed, he is about to leave when he hears whispers. It is Taiyyeb Ali, Salma's father, who is talking to a pretty woman who is demanding money from him. She is a nautch girl from a brothel. Akbar is amused and impressed; the old man has the heart of a romantic, he thinks to himself. He photographs them using a flash. When Ali looks up to see if there has been lightning, the woman, whose name is 'Bijli' (lightning), says it is nothing like what will happen if her wrath falls on him. He is worried and promises her money the next day.

Akbar sees some possibilities in this incident and the next day gathers a group of hijras to sing with him and embarrass his girlfriend's father. 'Taiyyeb Ali is an enemy of love,' he sings and drops hints about his mistress. The old man is incensed and pays off a bunch of thugs to beat up Akbar.

Akbar lands in the hospital with bruises. His friend Anthony, who believes in direct action, physically picks up Taiyyeb Ali from his shop and carries him to the hospital along with a Qazi to get Akbar and Salma married right then and there. But Akbar refuses, saying he does not believe in violence and is not going to marry his sweetheart by force. An irritated Anthony walks out of the hospital.

Over at Kishen Lal's house, Jenny is getting ready to step out for a date with Anthony when her muscled bodyguard Zebesco stops her. 'You cannot go out,' he says and tells her that he is going to marry her. 'You bastard,' she screams at him. He then calls up Robert, informing him that he has his daughter in his custody but will let him see her only if he agrees to them getting married. Robert demurs initially but then agrees. Zebesco asks him to come to Kishen's house but just then hears Kishen's car coming in the driveway.

Tying up Jenny with a rope, Zebesco tells Kishen that his daughter has gone to meet her boyfriend. But when Kishen leaves, he notices the blinds on the upper floor being shaken; it is Jenny who is using her feet to manipulate them to send a signal. The shrewd Kishen comes back into the house, holds a gun to Zebesco's head and applies chloroform to his face; Zebesco faints. Just as Kishen and Jenny are leaving, Robert comes with his cronies.

Kishen drives away speedily. Further down the road Akbar and Anthony are out on a leisurely drive when suddenly they see Kishen's car with Jenny drive past. Kishen tells Jenny to get out of the car and hide while he distracts Robert and his gang, who will chase him. The goons drive past Jenny, who is hiding under a huge tree, but when she shrieks upon seeing a snake, they spot her in their rear-view mirror and double back. Jenny runs through nearby fields, the bad guys chasing after her. Kishen too turns back and follows them. Jenny, tired after all that running, collapses near a scarecrow. The thugs approach her, but the scarecrow comes to life and beats them up—it is Anthony!

The other car crashes into Kishen's and overturns it. Kishen falls out of the car, injured, and is spotted by Akbar. Robert tries to run over Kishen but Akbar uses his vintage car to foil that attempt, causing Robert's car to swerve and fall into water. Akbar takes Kishen to the same hospital and the same bed which he was using till recently and the doctor advises a quick operation.

Back at the gangsters' den, Zebesco reminds Robert of his promise to give Jenny's hand to him. Robert pooh-poohs it, and Zebesco takes him to a room where he has held Albert captive— Albert, the identical twin of Robert, who works in London as a banker and is as honest as Robert is crooked. 'Let me marry Jenny,' says Zebesco, 'and I will arrange for you to go back to London in disguise to start a new life. I will "take care" of the real Albert.' Zebesco also tells Robert to visit local hospitals to see where Kishen Lal has been admitted; that could lead them to Jenny.

Robert locates Kishen and manages to get inside the operation theatre. He wants to know where he can find Jenny, but Kishen is unconscious. He orders the doctor, Salma, to revive Kishen. Robert also sees a locket of Santoshi Maa on Kishen and snatches it, believing it to be the source of Kishen's luck and strength. Meanwhile, Bharti lands up at the hospital and wants to give flowers to Akbar, but is told by the nurse that the 'patient' in that bed has been taken for emergency surgery. Bharti knocks on the door of the operation theatre, insisting on giving the flowers. When she comes in, Robert recognizes her and mutters, 'This is Kishen Lal's wife.' Salma hears this.

Robert takes Bharti with him in his car, but at

one corner the car swerves and both the driver and Robert are injured. Bharti gets out of the car and starts running away. She is drawn towards some music—it is Akbar singing a qawwali at a shrine to Saibaba of Shirdi, the Sufi mystic revered by millions of people. She moves towards it with Robert and his flunkey chasing her. They are prevented from entering the shrine by a cobra with an open hood. Akbar sings the praises of Saibaba who can right any wrong and as the song rises to a crescendo, two tiny shafts of light emanate from the eyes of the statue and move towards Bharti, touching her eyes. Suddenly she can see and her first vision is that of her three young sons calling her.

She tells Akbar that she is being followed. He takes her home to meet his foster-father who immediately recognizes her as the woman he had given a lift to that fateful night twenty-two years ago. She sees a picture of the little boy the man had picked up the same evening and recognizes the kid as her youngest son. It is Akbar. An emotional reunion follows.

A fire is raging in the house of Taiyyeb Ali. His mistress has taken her revenge. Both Ali and

Salma are trapped inside the house, the flames raging around them. Akbar comes there and tries to enter but is stopped by the crowds. He gets to a nearby terrace, ties a rope round his waist, swings into the burning house and bravely rescues both father and daughter. Taiyyeb Ali gives his blessings to the couple. Salma tells Akbar she has seen his father. Akbar rushes home and informs his mother and they head to the hospital, but Kishen Lal has already gone.

Akbar heads to the police station and files a missing person complaint. The inspector, who happens to be Amar, finds the name Kishen Lal of Bandra Koliwada familiar; it rings a bell in his mind. He goes to the neighbourhood and looks around. He recalls something dimly; a house, a hole in the ground, some digging. This is where he had hidden the toy gun, which his father had brought for him twenty-two years ago. His father Kishen Lal is also in the same place right then. He had come there to warn an employee of his who was treating his family badly. Kishen sees a police inspector and hides in his old house, from where he watches as Amar digs into the ground and finds that old gun. 'How did you know there was a gun there?' Kishen Lal asks Amar. 'I had hidden it here,' replies Amar. Kishen Lal immediately understands and reveals himself to his son. Another reunion.

Anthony is getting a wedding dress tailored for Jenny from Akbar's foster-father. After the measurements are taken, Anthony and Jenny leave and he drops her at the church. The priest during his sermon announces that his ward, Anthony, whom he found outside the church door twenty-two years ago is getting married and the bride is right there in the congregation. Jenny is thrilled; she rushes to inform Kishen Lal that she knows who his son is, but is cut off before she can give all the details. Robert is standing there and forcibly takes Jenny away. The priest stops Robert but Robert is not to be stopped today; he flashes his knife and the priest is dead. Jenny is bundled into a van and this is observed by Lakshmi who climbs unseen into the van too. Little does she realize that she has been spotted by her stepbrother who is with the goons. Both the girls are taken to Robert's lair.

Back at the church—Anthony comes back, smartly dressed in a new white suit and finds the priest kneeling at the altar. Unaware of all that has happened, Anthony launches into a monologue in which he promises that from now on there will be no illegal rackets, no fighting, no drinking. He will go straight. When the priest does not answer, Anthony touches him and discovers he is dead. Anthony is distraught and appeals to Jesus to let him know who did this. A locket with Santoshi Maa's picture on it drops from the priest's hand. Recalling where he had seen it last—around Kishen Lal's neck—Anthony lands up at the latter's home and at knife point questions him about the locket. Kishen tells him it had been snatched from him by Robert who was trying to find out the whereabouts of Jenny. Anthony is surprised to know that Jenny is Robert's daughter. Kishen further tells him that by a strange twist of fate, his enemy's daughter wants to marry his own son who got lost twenty-two years ago. Anthony takes out a tattered letter that he has preserved for twenty-two years—the same letter that Bharti had written to Kishen. It becomes clear that Anthony is indeed Kishen and Bharti's son. Reunion number three takes place.

Zebesco is at Akbar's shop asking about the

dress being made for Jenny. He wants it right away. Abkar smells a rat. He says he will come to the bride's house and do the final fitting there. Akbar disguises himself as an old tailor and sets out with Zebesco. When he asks to go back to get some material from his home, they refuse and ask him to write a list, which he does, in Urdu, so that only his beloved, Salma, can understand. In that he asks her to come and send out a message to Amar and Anthony. Jenny meanwhile is refusing to wear her bridal gown, despite the entreaties of Lakshmi.

Salma comes to Robert's den and both Amar and Anthony get the message and also land up at the same place, the first dressed up as a one-man band and the other as a priest. The three of them first sing a song and, when they are finally exposed as frauds, fight the goons. Robert is thrown in jail as is Kishen Lal. The family is united.

3

Making the Film

As word spread in the industry that Manmohan Desai was now making a fourth film in the year, his peers and others, as is the norm in the business, scoffed at everything—the name, the idea and the fact that he had taken three superstars in it. Even the female leads were big names: Neetu Singh, a regular co-star (and later wife) of Rishi Kapoor; Parveen Babi and Shabana Azmi, who was to be Vinod Khanna's love interest. The first reaction in the industry is usually to pick holes in a project; often it is borne out of envy, especially when a producer has managed to sign up top stars.

The choice of Azmi was a bit surprising, even

if she was working in Desai's other film, *Parvarish*. An alumnus of the Film and Television Institute of India, she had become one of the key actors in the Indian 'new wave' cinema, making her debut in *Ankur*, a film about rural exploitation. Her portfolio consisted mainly of small-budget, art-house films which had made her popular among critics and discerning audiences but which did not translate into mass recognition.

The two worlds of art films and mainstream commercial films did not meet or intersect and both viewed each other with wariness, if not hostility. The directors of 'art' films scoffed at the masala films, calling them lowbrow and exploitative; the latter returned the compliment, declaring the new-wave directors as self-indulgent pseudo-intellectuals, a dig at the fact that many of these films did not do well at the box office. Actors and even technicians belonged squarely in one camp or the other. The lines would eventually get blurred, as more and more new-wave directors, conscious of the need for box-office success, began to use big stars in their films, but in the mid-1970s, the two streams were mutually exclusive.

Shabana Azmi had made tentative crossings to

the other side, but was seen as firmly entrenched in the art world. Yet she was excited to get this offer.

'I had already done more than half of *Parvarish* with Manji and loved his no-nonsense, unabashed love for all things illogical but with a strong emotional content. His favourite film was *Kunwara Baap* and he would weep copiously whilst describing the climax. I remember Manji came to meet me at Ranjit Studios where I was shooting and said that he had decided to produce his first film and wanted me in it. He went on to add that it was about three brothers and while Vinod Khanna's character was a police officer who didn't need a leading lady opposite him, Vinod would have insisted on one because the other two stars did! So he had created a part for me. It was no great shakes, he admitted, but he wanted me to do it because it was his first film as producer. I loved his honesty and said yes without even listening to the story.'

This faith in Desai's abilities was evident in most people who worked with him. Ketan Desai recalls Bachchan telling him that working with Manmohan Desai meant surrendering to him.

'Either say yes to everything he says, or don't work with him.' There were lapses in logic and leaps of faith required of the audiences, but Desai would somehow manage them—that was the confidence that most of his actors had.

'We were not allowed to ask him questions. His stock reply used to be, "This is not a Satyajit Ray film. You do because I tell you." There was no question of preparing for the part,' remembers Bachchan. (For Desai, Satyajit Ray was a metaphor for seriousness and authenticity which had no place in Desai's world view.) The 'don't ask me any questions, just follow my instructions' bit is something that everyone who was interviewed for this book confirmed; they talked about it with affection and awe, even if some of them might have had their reservations.

Desai was also particular about the character actors he chose. The supporting cast in a film can often mar it and in a movie studded with the biggest names of the day, it would have been tempting to compromise on the rest to save costs, if nothing else. But Desai made a special effort to bring in veterans who he thought would add that extra something to their parts—Nirupa Roy, Pran,

Mukri and Jeevan—people he had a rapport with. As anyone who has seen *Amar Akbar Anthony* will testify, these actors were excellent and added tremendous value to the film.

While Pran was already a legend and Roy had by then become the most well-known screen mother—her role in *Deewaar* had catapulted her to the top of the maternal league—honourable mention must also be made of Yusuf Khan, the muscle-bound, well-coiffed, platform-shoes-wearing Zebesco. Yusuf, who hailed from Bangalore, had acted in quite a few Hindi films before this, usually uncredited and in bit roles. He made a small impact in *Bombay to Goa*, playing a boxer who challenges Mehmood to a duel, but *Amar Akbar Anthony* firmly put him in the spotlight as a reliable villain's henchman. Desai gave him generous screen time, a chance to act with big stars (and to beat up one of them, Amitabh Bachchan) and a memorable name, Zebesco, which stuck to him from then on. Tragically, he died at an early age.

While Prayag Raaj had written the screenplay, Desai signed up Kader Khan to write the dialogues. Khan is one of the more fascinating characters of

Hindi cinema to emerge in the 1970s. Though many film buffs will remember him as the man who played some colourful, even crude characters, first in the Hindi films from south India in the 1980s and later in films starring Govinda, he comes with a fine intellectual pedigree. He began life as a college lecturer who in his spare time acted on the stage. He grew up in the middle of Mumbai's notorious red-light area of Kamathipura, and kept his sanity, he says, by reading works by the great writers like Chekhov and Gorky. 'My teachers saved me,' he says humbly.

His reputation as a playwright and actor had begun to spread in the early 1970s and the producers of *Jawani Diwani* had commissioned him to write the dialogues at the princely sum of Rs 500. In 1973, Desai took him on as an additional dialogue writer. Khan recalls, 'He was a very frank kind of person. He told me, "I have had some problems with some Muslim writers. I will try you and if your stuff is bad, I will throw it in the gutter." "And if my work is good?" I asked him. "Then I will carry you on my back," he replied. Within days, I had written some lines and took them to his home in Khetwadi. He was

playing cricket with the kids. He muttered
something and I told him that he had given me a
gaali. "I am good at lip-reading," I told him.'
(This lip-reading bit was used by Desai later in his
film *Naseeb*.)

Khan continues, 'I showed him what I had
written. He became mad with joy; *junoon sa ho
gaya unko*. Then he became very emotional. I had
just been given Rs 25,000 for *Khel Khel Mein*,
which was already too much for me. He scoffed at
it. "From today you get Rs 1.25 lakh," he said.
He got me a portable Toshiba TV set and a gold
bracelet from inside his house. I became his regular
writer from then on.'

Khan wrote a few dialogues about each character
that were then used for the muhurat shot. (The
muhurat, or auspicious occasion, is a very
important event for a film; it not only launches
the movie, but is also an occasion to call financiers,
journalists and well-wishers to show the clout of
the film-maker.)

Desai's faith in Khan was not misplaced. The
strength of *Amar Akbar Anthony* lies in the fact
that each character speaks differently in keeping
with his or her background. Thus, while Akbar,

being a romantic qawwali singer, is flowery in his speech, Amar the inspector is matter-of-fact, and Anthony uses Mumbai street patois, in which grammar is often mangled. Consider the scene where Anthony, while tripping a fugitive Robert who is carrying a box full of gold bars, says: '*Aisa to life mein aadmi do bar heech bhagta hai—ya to race mein ya police ke case mein.*' ('An individual runs this fast only twice—either in a race or if he is escaping from the police.') The tone is flip, the lingo is strictly Mumbai-street and the lines are appropriate. They also establish Anthony's insouciance and his control over the situation. Not surprisingly, the audience loved it.

For the lyrics and music, Desai chose the popular combination of the day, Anand Bakshi and Laxmikant-Pyarelal. Bakshi, a former army man turned songwriter, had the ability to write songs in everyday language and had collaborated with the duo in several films. Laxmikant-Pyarelal were the most in-demand team in the 1970s, their name alone a guarantee of success. They had worked with Desai in only one film, *Roti*, but had known him since his *Chhalia* days, when both the musicians were working for Kalyanji-Anandji.

'Manmohan Desai had an interesting way of telling a story,' Pyarelal remembers, sitting in his sea-facing house in Bandra's tony Mount Mary area. A piano stands in the corner. 'He acted out the roles and described the characters of the three heroes. We then worked closely with Anand Bakshi and for each of the heroes used different phrases in the song "*Humko tumse ho gaya hai pyar kya karein*". For Amar it was "*Ram kasam*", for Akbar "*Khuda gawah*" and for Anthony, "*God promise*".' The song had three male singers—Mohammed Rafi, Mukesh and Kishore Kumar—but Lata Mangeshkar sang for all the three female actors. 'Lataji is so versatile that she changed her style for each of the three actresses. I always say that she could have even done the male voices,' says Pyarelal. The musician contributed to the film in another way too. 'The original name of Amitabh Bachchan's character was Anthony Fernandes. I requested Manji to change it to Anthony Gonsalves, after my guruji.' Anthony Gonsalves was one of India's leading violinists and music arrangers who had moved to Goa after retirement. Few will disagree that it was an inspired change— Anthony Gonsalves is a far more musical name.

Desai had a team of technicians who worked with him on several projects, but none was closer to him than Peter Pereira, a veteran cameraman whom he had known for decades. Now in his eighties, Pereira leads a retired life in Mumbai. Surrounded by his trophies, many of them for Desai's films (including *Amar Akbar Anthony*), Pereira reminisces about working for Desai: 'He used to call me his lucky mascot. I first worked for him in *Sachaa Jhutha*, though I had known him and had even worked with his guru Babubhai Mistry.' *Roti* followed, and the bond between director and cameraman grew. Pereira says Desai had a sequence in mind for *Roti* in which a woman is stoned by angry villagers. 'I told him the story of Mary Magdalene and how Jesus had said, "Let him who has not sinned cast the first stone." A song on those lines was then written ("*Yaar hamari baat suno*").'

Pereira was thus his Anthony and Kader Khan his Akbar to advise him on the nuances of both the communities. Desai was extremely sensitive to some community concerns; he asked Pereira whether it would be okay to show a murder in a church. 'I said it should be fine. See, Robert, the man who kills the priest, is a lapsed Catholic.'

Yet, Desai had to contend with angry Catholics who felt that the film was uncomplimentary to Christians. The Christian community has often bristled at the stereotypical way in which its members are shown—either as kindly priests or as drunks and bootleggers. This film had both. An angry debate broke out in the community press, chiefly in the pages of the *Examiner*, the Catholic community newspaper from Mumbai.

Father Joe Pereira, a well-known priest of the city, intervened in the furore. 'The controversy had a double angle—first, the bad projection of the Christian community in all Bollywood movies. Second, this particular film,' he says. Though Anthony was not ridiculed and his image in the film was 'fair and respectful', some community members were upset at a scene set in Anthony's liquor bar which had a picture of Jesus Christ. But the priest pointed out that the cameraman, Peter Pereira, who was greatly admired among his co-religionists, would not do anything to denigrate the religion. The controversy died down soon enough.

Peter Pereira used to sit in on all story sessions, along with the scriptwriters and assistants. 'Everyone contributed to the discussion.'

Locations had to be finalized for various shoots. Pereira suggested the lovely Mount Mary church on top of a small hill in Bandra. But the indoor scenes were shot in Don Bosco church in Matunga, another part of Mumbai. 'It could be done only between 3 and 4.30 p.m., because the light changed indoors after that and it became a bit dark.' The fight scene between Amar and Anthony was filmed over two days in Bandra Koliwada and to ensure things went smoothly, local toughs were engaged to maintain peace and silence.

Pereira recalls that Desai and he agreed that all indoor scenes would be shot with very bright lights. This suited the sunny mood of the film but also helped in focusing on the stars. There was no room for darkness in the Manmohan Desai scheme of things. Sadness and melancholy were alien to the Desai brand of film-making and dimly lit scenes were therefore a strict no-no. If you have the stars, why not show them in full glory? Thus not only the stars but also the backdrops were fully lit. Pereira used to coordinate with the art director to make sure that there were enough places to position the bright lights.

There was another, practical reason for this

brightness policy. 'Manji told me that his films were meant not only for the big cities but also for the *chavanni* cinemas in the small towns. Their projection equipment is old and run-down; a darkly shot film will not look good on the screen.'

Like everyone else, Pereira too remembers Manmohan Desai as an easy and generous person to work with, as long as you did not question his instructions and his weird logic. Desai would use what can only be described as 'colourful' language, replete with words and phrases picked up on the streets where he had grown up. Many of his co-workers fondly remember his tendency to cuss, but most emphasize that this was done without malice or anger. His style was frenetic and fast, and he expected his actors and technicians to just follow his direction and keep their doubts to themselves. 'I would go on the set, be given the scene in the make-up room, mug up the lines and face the camera,' says Shabana Azmi. No discussion on motivation or method. It helped that he had top-class professionals working for him.

For all his street-smartness, Desai was a bit of a puritan. He did not touch liquor, except on one occasion. Rishi Kapoor talks of the time when after a good day of shooting Desai—a teetotaller—announced he felt like having a drink. It was a blazing hot afternoon and after a drink or two he passed out. But Kapoor and a few others kept on drinking till late at night with the inevitable results the next day. 'We cursed him for setting us off on a long drinking spree.'

The story and structure of the film being such, the dates of all the big stars were rarely required at the same time. Except for the climax, the big names did not come together on the screen. That particular shoot, when the title song was filmed, required a month-long stint at the now-defunct Ranjit Studios.

Inevitably, tensions did crop up. The climax schedule went beyond its deadline, leading to some chaos with dates. Kapoor had to rush off to Delhi for another shoot which was to be done with the Republic Day parade as the backdrop. Since his part in *Amar Akbar Anthony* was to wind up by 20 January, he felt there was enough leeway, but things did not work out according to plan. 'Manji's shift did not end and he asked me to stay back. I had to refuse; you can't get the Republic Day parade again, you know. He was equally adamant since he had the dates of the other stars. It was an impasse. He threatened my secretary that he would turn me into a parrot in the climax scene—this is Manmohan Desai, remember, he knew special effects and he could do anything in his film. Finally, they shot my parts separately, just playing on a bongo and the accordion in the fight scene. In some of those shots he used a double, since I had already left the set; you can see the guy looking down to hide his face. I also don't actually fight in the film except hitting a bad guy once and not before I apologize to Allah by raising my hands. These shots were used as cutaways in the film, while the others are fighting!'

Luck worked in Desai's favour. The censor rules of the time disallowed the depiction of violence on the screen for more than 90 feet of film continuously. So directors used to deploy all kinds of tricks, using cutaways before returning to the *dhishum-dhishum*; Kapoor's bongo playing came in quite handy and got many laughs in the film. Sticking to the tone of the film—jokey but not ridiculous—the fights were funny in parts but followed the template of filmi fights of the era.

After the sidekicks were beaten up, the main villain, in this case Robert, had to be bashed up personally by the hero. In this case, he was hammered by both Amar and Anthony, in their capacity as the elder brothers, though Akbar too got in a blow. The fight scene offers the final cathartic resolution to a story, the literal climax of a three-hour ride during which the lead actors have been put through many travails by the dastardly villain. One kick on his backside pushes Robert into the same police cell as his nemesis Kishen, who after all was a smuggler. But he is all smiles as he tells his wife Bharti not to cry—she had got her whole family back. The young sons beam with their respective girlfriends.

It is clear, however, that the real star of the film is Bachchan. Though the others had fairly good and meaty roles and brought their own lustre to the high-wattage film, Bachchan was much bigger than any of them at the time. Kapoor acknowledges it by saying, 'We all ran 100 metres, while he had to sprint only seventy-five.' Nonetheless, he says, he stood up to the superstar and established his own mark on the role. He got five opportunities to sing and his character Akbar, with his skull

cap, his netted vest, his transparent shirt and his
paan-stained lips are all remembered fondly even
today.

The shooting of the film proceeded at a furious
clip and was over almost before anyone realized it.
Ketan Desai, who was in school but already
showing an interest in his father's business, was a
general gopher around the sets. One day his father
told him to tally all the shots of *Amar Akbar
Anthony* that were canned. The Manmohan Desai
style of doing a bit of this and a bit of that meant
that he had not kept track of where each film
stood. Young Ketan did an audit and realized that
the shooting of the film *Amar Akbar Anthony* was
now complete. His father refused to believe him
and asked him to double-check. The first
assessment was confirmed; Desai, busy with several
projects at the same time, had finished the shooting
part of *Amar Akbar Anthony* and the film was now
ready to be edited. It is often said that in the
Hindi film business no one has a complete script
before he sets out to make a film; it's all done as
they go along. The Desai style apparently was
even more chaotic. He had no clue that he had
finished his job, even though he was a meticulous

planner before he came on the sets to direct a scene. One can almost imagine the scene of film 'A' landing up in film 'B'. But of course Desai had complete clarity in his head about what he wanted his film to look like and had shot according to the plan he had devised. There was method in that madness.

Yet he was nervous about the film when it was due for release. Would the audiences accept a film like this? It was his first production—the other films had opened well, but this was his own baby. It had to succeed. Would anyone show up? He needn't have worried. On the Monday before the film opened, there were queues outside the advance booking windows. It looked like Manmohan Desai would have the last laugh.

4

Spicing It Up:
The Masala Film

Amitabh Bachchan, top-hatted and monocled, emerging from a giant Easter egg. The four-foot-four-inch comedian Mukri, with a glamorous courtesan as mistress. A blind Nirupa Roy recovering her eyesight by divine miracle and without resorting to surgery. All in a day's work for the madcap genius Manmohan Desai, the masala maestro, the maharaja of madness, the lord of the lost-and-found story, the man with the common touch. In his hands, old ideas acquired a new flavour and energy and hackneyed themes appeared fresh. Logic was often a casualty, but strangely, the coincidences appeared believable and the flights of imagination were somehow credible. Yours was not to ask, but just see and enjoy. The punters loved it, and to Desai that was the ultimate accolade. He did not care for the critics or the highbrows—in fact, as he told one critic, he got scared when they gave his films good reviews. He understood the formula.

The 'formula' is integral to Hindi films. What exactly it is no one can really tell you, but everyone knows its essential elements. A bit of this—emotion, humour, action, melodrama—and a bit of that—songs, fights, dances, foreign locations—all sprinkled in judicious quantities throughout the film. But even if it sounds simple, it is not a template as dull and lazy film-makers often think. It requires intelligence to make the perfect formula film which gives the viewer the all-important feeling of 'paisa vasool' or money's worth.

The dismissive criticism of the typical Hindi film as being little more than film-making by numbers is not without merit. Most film-makers do aim to make films as per the formula to achieve box-office success. This is no different from what happens in the big Hollywood studios where the ultimate goal is profit maximization by making genre films—romcoms, blockbusters, buddy cop dramas.

The Hindi formula is not a static one; it changes from season to season, year to year, generation to generation. Some features are constant—filial love, emotionalism, comedy, songs—and these have remained the same for decades and may never change, but there are significant shifts as audience tastes transform.

The trick is to get the mixture right. Like a good chef, a director has to know what spices to use and at what points in the cooking process he must sprinkle them. At the same time, the director must not forget that mainstream Indian audiences essentially want comfort food when they walk into a cinema hall. Too much experimentation can put them off. New recipes are all very well, but for guaranteed commercial success, sticking to the familiar is usually the best option.

Manmohan Desai was the perfect chef. He took old, clichéd formulas and breathed new life into them. His admirers said he had the ability to get into the mind of the viewer. In the pre-multiplex days, when films were shown in large, thousand-seater single-screen theatres, they had to run for twenty-five consecutive weeks at least to be legitimately called hits; anything less than that was an average grosser and anything beyond that became a blockbuster. To achieve that status was not easy. Films had to have 'repeat value' and had to appeal to the masses of different demographics, genders and linguistic backgrounds. A film that appealed to Punjabis could well bomb in western, central and eastern India; the south, with its own strong film industry, was an even more difficult bastion to penetrate. A movie with strong emotional appeal among women could put off children, teenagers and single young men. Women were likely to give the hard-core actioner a miss. The family film—usually a weepy one with bits of comedy and no vulgarity—was a safer bet, but not always. Film-makers therefore tended to put in a bit of everything, which is what Desai did too.

The 1965 film *Waqt*, directed by Yash Chopra, was the first film packed with big stars of the time. And like *Amar Akbar Anthony*, *Waqt* too had three brothers separated in an earthquake soon after birth. Then, in the 1970s, after a gap of a decade or so, Bombay film-makers rediscovered the multi-starrer and films such as *Sholay* and *Deewaar* were made; the collective star power made them an attractive proposition. Producers realized that two or three or more big stars could bring in bigger audiences and after a few of these films succeeded, there was a scramble to sign up every available star.

For *Amar Akbar Anthony*, Manmohan Desai selected not one, two or three, but six big names and then added the top character actors of the time, like Pran, Jeevan, Nirupa Roy and Mukri. All of which made *Amar Akbar Anthony* a true multi-starrer in the *Sholay* mould. 'Remember, all the three heroes of the time were top names of the era. A remake of *Amar Akbar Anthony* will work only if you took three of the biggest names of today,' says Rishi Kapoor.

Yet, hiring top stars was one thing; giving them substantive roles, punchy lines and adequate screen time was quite another. What is more, each of these stars had a particular persona, an image in the minds of film lovers. Experimenting once in a while was acceptable, but upending their image was not a recommended course of action. But Desai was no ordinary director. He had a plan and worked towards it. No one could change his mind once he was convinced. It is his handling of the superstar cast and ensuring that each one is optimally utilized that give *Amar Akbar Anthony* its special feel though inevitably, one or two stars felt short-changed in the end. Shabana Azmi says there was a 'lot of disappointment' that she had acted in the film. '"What is Shabana Azmi doing in this film" was a common public reaction, and they asked that only of me, not of Parveen or Neetu. There was many a protest because my role was so small.' In the end it did her no harm however; it nudged her closer to the mainstream where she went on to become a star of distinction. But it is true that *Amar Akbar Anthony* is a 'male' film, where the women are fillers to provide glamour and romancing opportunities to the heroes. All the three women are saved by their menfolk when they land in trouble—Salma is rescued by Akbar from a fire, Anthony beats up bad guys who are after Jenny, and Inspector Amar takes Lakshmi out of her wretched domestic existence and the torture heaped on her by her stepmother and stepbrother.

Too much realism in cinema was something

that film-makers like Manmohan Desai deliberately stayed away from. This was in keeping with their firm belief that the viewing public—the front-benchers—did not want to see their lives reflected on the screen. They came to fulfil their fantasies and to seek out new ones. They wanted their stars larger than life, dressed well, mouthing bombastic lines. They wanted glamorous sets and lovely locations. They wanted emotions, and that too supersized ones; a fair representation of the grim realities of their own lives was certainly not what they desired.

Thus, the 1970s potboiler was all about action, melodrama, comedy—an all-in-one portmanteau which kept the audience engaged throughout. The age of pure romance, as witnessed in the 1960s, had faded away and Rajesh Khanna, the last of the soft-looking romantic star, had been replaced by the angry and intense Amitabh Bachchan, who did not sing, romance or even smile.

Bachchan had made his name in films like *Zanjeer*, *Deewaar* and *Sholay* and had brought about a paradigm shift in the industry. His Angry Young Man films were focused—there was no time for romance and certainly none for singing or dancing. In his early landmark films—*Zanjeer, Deewaar, Namak Haraam*—he did not ever sing on screen. However, by the time he began acting in *Amar Akbar Anthony*, the age of the angry hero was dying out.

The Emergency was on while the film was being made but in any case Desai was not a 'political' film-maker and had little or no truck with the real world around him. His was not a realistic look at the India of his time; if at all that India intruded, it was by way of the more abstract ideals like unity in diversity. He was au fait with current trends to the extent that the villains in his film, as was the norm at the time, were smugglers, identified by official India as the enemies of the state. If he had made the film today, the bad guys would have been terrorists or politicians.

Audiences were moving away from the vengeance-seeking hero. Now they wanted a bit of everything. Having come out of a traumatic nineteen months of oppressive state control, which had been preceded by several years of hardship and political turmoil, they were ready to let their hair down. Film-makers like Prakash Mehra and

Manmohan Desai had figured it out. Both were directing Bachchan—and other stars—in pure entertainers, three-hour extravaganzas which moved at a breathless pace and took the viewer on a fun-filled ride of good music, charged emotions and a few laughs and thrills. The Angry Young Man had quietly faded into the background; Bachchan was in two Desai film released in 1977—*Amar Akbar Anthony* and *Parvarish*—and both were vastly different from what he had become famous for.

Amar Akbar Anthony therefore is a fairly typical confection of the time. It is a series of well-crafted set pieces, all seamlessly fitted together to form an entertaining whole. Scriptwriter Anjum Rajabali, who has written several successful films such as *Ghulam* and *Rajneeti*, calls them 'episodes'. 'There is an episodic quality to the film, almost as if Desai asked his writers to come up with some highlight sequences and then built the story around them. "Give me a sequence first and then we shall see how best to connect them to the main story," he could have told them.'

Yet, though there are several familiar elements—clichés, if you will—that are found in other films, Desai tweaked and presented them in his own unique style.

The perfect gentleman: Amitabh Bachchan emerging from a giant Easter Egg is one of the most iconic images of Indian cinema. It was the brainchild of Manmohan Desai, who was always on the lookout for outlandish sequences to please the crowds.

The tapori with a golden heart: Anthony is a street-smart bootlegger who talks with his fists but also yearns for a girl who will get the violins playing in his head. The comic role in *Amar Akbar Anthony* effectively broke the mould of Bachchan as the Angry Young Man.

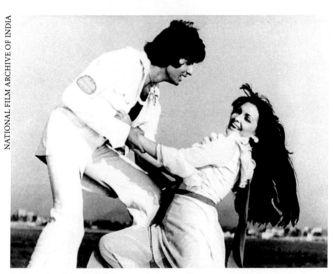

Romancing his sweetheart: Bachchan and Parveen Babi were a popular on-screen pair in the 1970s.

Clash of the titans: A fight scene between two top heroes has to be handled carefully—neither can be shown as tougher than the other. Desai came up with a unique solution and Bachchan, despite being beaten up, had the audience rooting for him.

All for love: Akbar the qawwal mocks his lady love's father who then sets goons on to him to beat him up.

Love heals all: Dr Salma rushes to her beau Akbar after he is beaten up.

Maternal love: Nirupa Roy was the mother of all mothers in Hindi films of the 1970s. Here, she comes to the police station where one son is an inspector, the other in jail. The film was full of such piquant moments where the family members keep meeting each other without knowing of their relationship.

The men who scripted the madness: Prayag Raaj and Kader Khan wrote the screenplay and dialogue for Manmohan Desai's films in the 1970s and 1980s.

The star and the star director: Manmohan Desai got the biggest stars of the time to act in his films, but was also a bona fide star himself.

A cast of colourful characters: One strength of Desai's films was the supporting actors, such as Pran, Jeevan and Yusuf Khan.

Not so fast: Pran modelled his look on Abraham Lincoln.

The king of Anthonywadi: The role of Anthony the bootlegger was based on a man who brewed illicit liquor in the lanes near Manmohan Desai's family home.

Musical climax: The end of the film involved all the actors, a difficult exercise given how busy everyone was. Desai had to resort to some editing tricks to achieve the desired result.

Stars all: It was the time of multi-starrer films and the poster reflects that.

The qawwalis in the film are a good example. The qawwali form of singing goes back several hundred years and is practised by Sufi singers to express their love and devotion to the almighty. These kinds of songs had more or less faded from Hindi films in the 1970s and were seen as a throwback to the previous decade, when many 'Muslim socials' were made, primarily to woo the Muslim audience. The late 1950s and 1960s were the heyday of this genre of cinema with an 'Islamic' backdrop; they were set usually in Lucknow, the epicentre of a particular kind of formalized Muslim culture. Such films invariably had a qawwali.

Desai must have sensed an opportunity here— Akbar, the youngest brother was a qawwal and thus it made sense to give him several such numbers. In one of them ('*Pardah hai pardah*'), Akbar sings to his burqa-clad lady-love Salma (Neetu Singh), sending her not-so-cryptic messages while she sits in the audience with her stern father; in another ('*Shirdiwale Saibaba*'), he appeals to the sufi mystic Saibaba to answer the prayers of his devotees. The saint duly performs a miracle and restores eyesight to Akbar's mother Bharti.

This 'miracle' was conceived and executed on

the screen by Ramesh Meer, then a young graduate from the Film and Television Institute of India, the famous school that has given the industry many fine technicians and actors. Till then, Desai was working with his one-time guru and mentor Babubhai Mistry, the father of special effects in India, but the latter's skills were now looking jaded and tacky. Desai needed newer ideas for his films and commissioned Meer to create effects for one of his under-production films, *Chacha Bhatija*. 'Manji loved what I did and immediately embraced me, declaring that I would be his effects technician from then onwards.'

Meer, now a respected special effects veteran, says the two got along well. 'Manji had a style of communication all his own and you had to take it in your stride.' This is a reference to Desai's use of colourful street language that everyone had come to accept as part of his personality. 'But he used to leave me alone. Only once did he come on the sets of *Parvarish* and when he found me constantly trying to improve something, he shouted, "Do you think I am Satyajit Ray? Finish this and move on."'

While *Parvarish* and *Dharam Veer* demanded

many effects, there were barely a couple required for *Amar Akbar Anthony*. One shows Anthony seemingly walking on air in the song '*My name is Anthony Gonsalves*', which was executed by cameraman Peter Pereira. The other has Nirupa Roy getting her eyesight back thanks to the blessings of Shirdi Saibaba. Meer took a shot of the Saibaba statue and superimposed flames from two lamps on its eyes, which then moved and lodged themselves in Nirupa Roy's eyes. 'A simple enough task, though you must remember we had no computers and CGI in those days.' (A similar four-foot-high statue of Shirdi Saibaba sits in Meer's office today.)

With one stroke, Desai had given a hit song, pleased the millions of followers of Saibaba and also shown the power of filial love, to say nothing of solving a tricky point in the story of making the mother see again. The song—which Pyarelal says was added virtually at the last moment—was a highlight of the film, with audiences going back again and again to see it. In industry parlance, this is called 'repeat value', and it is much desired by producers, since it brings in more revenue. The fact that Akbar sang to an idol, which is forbidden by Islam, may have provoked comment here and there but did not result in any controversy; audiences can be forgiving if they know that the film-maker has no ulterior motives.

Nor did the fact that the so-called 'miracle' in the film was a far-fetched one bother anyone—it worked for the film, didn't it? There was a message in it too, that the love of a son combined with the power of a saint could achieve anything.

Rishi Kapoor, who sang the song in the film, is a bit more sceptical. 'Things like that were possible in those days. Today's audiences will not accept the scene; they are much more discerning and will laugh it off.'

Rajabali puts it in another way. 'Manmohan Desai had a pact with his audiences. You can have either logic or emotions, but not both. It was manipulative, but the audience knew that and as long as it was being entertained, it accepted those leaps of logic.'

Desai the conjurer had many other tricks up his sleeve. The way he handled the fights on screen, for example, is worth studying in some detail. The 'fight scene' is a crucial part of the typical Hindi film mix. It establishes the heroes' macho credentials, but also provides catharsis to the audience; wrongs must be set right and order must be restored to the world. More often than not, a typical commercial film of the era had three major fight scenes. One could be between the hero and sundry low-ranking goons, wherein he either saves a distraught damsel from distress or stops them from doing some other dastardly act. In any case, with judicious use of his fists and kicks, he despatches them forthwith, clearly showing himself to be physically and morally superior while also impressing the girl. The second such sequence comes in halfway through the film when the hero and the main villain come across each other. Here, the hero could get beaten up, either because he refuses to resist the blows being rained upon him or the bad guy is somehow advantaged, with greater muscle power on his side. This invokes pity among viewers and also begins building up resentment. Naturally, the hero is itching to avenge himself and the audience is restless that the bad guy seems to be getting away. The last reel or two therefore is devoted to the climactic fight where the villain gets his just deserts at the hands of the hero—who represents truth, justice and righteousness—and is caught by the cops and presumably locked away. The hero wins the girl and the equilibrium is established once again.

Desai was not satisfied with such simplistic story arcs, at least not for *Amar Akbar Anthony*. With three heroes and a whole panoply of villains, he had to come up with innovative ways of telling the story. And casting three top male stars in the film had its own problems; their personas demanded they each romance, sing and fight.

Arguably, the most difficult issue would have been the face-off between the two brothers Amar and Anthony. One was a cop, the other a bootlegger; it was inevitable that they clashed somewhere. This would also provide the opportunity to include some bombastic dialogue as well as dramatic tension; the two are on opposite sides of the law and do not know they are related, but the audience does. Both were big names of their times and manly heroes whom the audience expected to fight hard and win. Bachchan, as the top star of the 1970s, could obviously not lose a fight, but nor could Vinod Khanna, whose macho image depended on good fight scenes. 'Manji told me, I cannot have you hammering a police officer; he is the law,' says Bachchan.

What Desai came up with is the stuff of genius. There is a fair amount of banter between the two before the actual fight, as Amar questions Anthony and the latter replies in a flippant manner. The audience of course is in on the joke and the double entendre. But when Amar catches Anthony by the collar, the mood promptly changes. This is a snub and it will not do; a real film hero will not stand for anyone insulting him like this and Anthony makes sure Amar knows he is only tolerating it because the latter is a police officer.

The fight begins and Amar has an answer for every move Anthony makes. The tone and tenor of the fight are light-hearted though. In the end, both fall inside a hut from where chicken, goats and other such creatures rush out and finally Amar emerges, carrying Anthony on his shoulder. Clearly, Anthony has been bested. In the jail, Anthony grudgingly admits that he has never been beaten up like this before: '*Apun apna life mein itna maar nahin khaya,*' he tells the inspector, who ignores him. But then Desai lets Bachchan, clearly the bigger hero, salvage some respect: '*Tum humko das das mara. Apun tumko sirf do mara, lekin solid mara ke nahin?*' (You hit me several times. I just hit you twice, but they were solid blows, weren't they?) he asks Amar in typical Mumbai street lingo. The balance has been restored, because though the cop, who is also the elder brother, has prevailed, the other hero's honour has also been protected.

Many of the familiar tropes of Hindi cinema of the 1970s were deployed in the film, the most obvious one being 'lost and found'. The idea of children getting separated (willingly or otherwise) from their parents in childhood only to be discovered years later is as old as the Mahabharata—Kunti had to perforce let go of her son Karna, who then grew up away from his brothers, the Pandavas, and fought them in the great war.

In Hindi films, the earliest known example of this device being used was in *Kismet*, starring Ashok Kumar. The film, released in 1943, was a big hit, running for over three years in a single cinema in Kolkata and told the story of a thief who turns out to belong to a respectable family.

In the 1960s and 1970s, on-screen children

were getting lost and then found years later with amazing regularity. And Desai was at the vanguard of these lost-and-found tales; he raised what others had discovered before him to a fine art. In Desai's film *Dharam Veer*, two brothers are separated by the machinations of an evil uncle. Ditto in *Parvarish*, where the dacoit's son grows up to be a police officer while the police commissioner's son, mistaken in his belief that he is a dacoit's son, becomes a smuggler. The idea of three brothers getting separated was first tried out in *Waqt*, a blockbuster of the 1960s, and then repeated in *Yaadon Ki Baaraat* a decade later in which three brothers go in different directions when their parents are killed by a brutal gangster who fears that the father is an eyewitness to a murder. Though there was a superficial resemblance between the lost-and-found theme of *Yaadon Ki Baaraat* and *Amar Akbar Anthony*, the rest of the story and the treatment were totally different— the former was much darker and violent.

Amar Akbar Anthony is unarguably the final word on the lost-and-found formula, indeed the benchmark for all such stories; it would be difficult for anyone to make a film with that basic idea and not be compared with Desai's film. Not only does the entire family disperse, they also find each other in novel, interesting ways. Moreover, Desai worked out a series of permutations and combinations by which they meet all the time unaware of their relationship. You could argue that they are with each other more than they would have been had they been a normal family. The lines they speak inevitably drip with double meaning with words like bhai (used for a brother as well as a stranger), maaji (literally mother, but also used for a maternal, elderly lady) and baap (father) frequently used.

In the scene where Anthony is kidnapped by Kishen's men while on the way to the court from the jail, the two constantly talk to each other in double entendre:

'*Aap kaun hai, mai-baap?*' says Anthony.

'*Mai nahin, tumhara baap,*' replies Kishen.

'*Kuch khaoge?*' asks Kishen.

'Why not? *Agar baap khilayega toh beta* of course *khayega,*' comes the reply.

This goes on for some time.

Desai was nudging and winking at the audience which nudged and winked back. Kader Khan's crackling dialogue, which caught the flavour of the Mumbai patois accurately, added to the fun.

In a film full of memorable sequences, the one highlight that stands out is undoubtedly the 'mirror scene'. It is a variation on similar sequences in the Marx Brothers' *Duck Soup* and in *Kohinoor* which had Dilip Kumar in the lead. (Manmohan Desai would use it again in *Mard*.) But while the other two involved two actors, like in *Mard*, Bachchan's was a solo performance. And what a performance it was—in any montage of his best-ever scenes, this will surely find a place.

'Ah, the mirror scene,' says Bachchan, with a twinkle in his eye. 'It was done in an impromptu manner. I was shooting in RK Studios for two movies—*Parvarish* and *Amar Akbar Anthony*, both with Manji. I used to shoot one scene on one set, rush to the other one, change clothes, and shoot for the second movie. Manji was doing the same. There was a mirror scene planned but nothing had been discussed. He gave me some dialogues and went off. Suddenly, his assistants said, let us just shoot it while he is away. That was it. We set it up and I did it. I knew the dialogues but added a few lines of my own. It was all done in one take.

When Manji returned, we told him it had been done. I hope it went well, he said. Yes, we assured him. In those days you got to see the rushes after several weeks. The film had to be developed, processed and so on. After a month or so, while shooting the climax in Ranjit Studios, he asked to see the mirror scene. There was a small preview theatre and he sat there, watching in silence. He came out of the screening, sat down on the porch and looked at me and said, "From now on, you will be in every film of mine." I could see he was moved.'

The scene comes immediately after Bachchan's character is badly bashed up by the muscled Zebesco. Anthony Gonsalves, completely enamoured by Jenny, sings and dances to attract her attention at the Easter dance but his flirtatious behaviour irks Zebesco, her bodyguard. Once the song is over, Zebesco challenges Anthony to a fight; Anthony is drunk that evening and in his drunken haze sees not one but many Zebescos. At the time, Bachchan was the undisputed star of Hindi films and had developed a reputation for on-screen fights. He made them look credible. In any other normal filmy situation he could have comfortably taken on all the Zebescos and come out with not a hair out of place. Here, Desai had him reduced to pulp. It had to be explained away.

The drunk Anthony, after losing a rather comically choreographed fight, lands up at home and looks at his battered, bruised face in the mirror. He begins by berating the image for not listening to his warnings to never drink: 'If you were not drunk, would that fatty have ever bashed you? Tell me,' says Anthony. 'You are the man, Anthony, you can by yourself take on ten people at a time.' The star's essential machismo is established and the viewer gets the message—this was a special case. And when he declares, again to his face (and thus to himself), 'Look at yourself in the mirror, see what an idiot you look like.' The audience roars at the joke and his style of speaking. As much as Bachchan's convincing acting was the Mumbai lingo that he used with great panache throughout the film. (It is to the credit of the star that he let go of his image and agreed to getting bashed up in the film not once but twice over—once at the hands of Vinod Khanna and then at the hands of a villain's sidekick. And strangely enough, he had the audience eating out of his hand.)

He then tries to stick Band-Aid on his bruises, except that he does it on the mirror, or rather his image. The effect is unbelievably comical and still raises a laugh all these years later. We are lost in the moment, laughing as much with him as at him. Bachchan the tough, intense, brooding guy of *Deewaar*, etc., is now Bachchan the Everyman, still tough but vulnerable and definitely lovable. The whole thing is very believable; anyone who has made a fool of himself after a drinking binge knows exactly how it feels.

This is perhaps the only moment in the film when there is a hint of a character's inner life. It is a funny monologue, but a monologue nonetheless. In it, Anthony talks to himself, showing self-doubt and even self-loathing because not only did he get badly beaten up, it happened in front of the girl he loves. What will she think? That he is a weakling, a drunkard, a ne'er-do-well? It taps into his insecurities, though fortunately, it completely avoids self-pity. Anthony is upset, but only momentarily. We know that he will come out of it eventually, perhaps as early as the next morning. There is never any mention of it again and Anthony gets many opportunities to show Jenny what he is capable of. In any case, Zebesco turns out to be a traitor and behaves badly with Jenny (allowing her to say, 'you bastard', a licence that she as a Christian girl can take, apparently). We can thus see that the mirror scene is an 'item', an insert that is entertaining by itself and adds a bit to our understanding of the character but that could easily have been deleted without any loss to the overall story or pace.

Many other set pieces also stand out. The scene where Inspector Amar goes to his childhood home to search for the missing Kishen is one such. While roaming around the poor neighbourhood, he begins to recall small details. He remembers that he had buried a toy gun in the ground so that his other brothers could not find it; rushing there, the adult Amar begins digging and sure enough finds it. The father Kishen is watching all this and tells his son: 'You remember the gun your father gave you, but don't remember the father who gave it to you.' They embrace, full of emotion at having met after all the intervening years. Manmohan Desai knows it is a charged moment, but is also aware that it should not slow down the film. He moves quickly on to the next scene.

A special mention must be made of Desai's handling of the character actors. Often, filmmakers invest the least in them, thinking erroneously that they do not matter if the film has big stars. But the supporting cast are crucial. They enhance the film in many ways and are a good foil to the lead actors. A bad character actor can destroy a scene; a good one can strengthen it. Each of the actors Desai chose for the crucial character roles came with a fine acting pedigree.

Pran, one of Hindi film screen's best known villains played the driver-turned-smuggler with aplomb. He is one of Hindi cinema's most durable and enduring actors and had nearly 175 films under his belt by then. Outright villainy, funny villainy, comedy, he had done them all and had successfully transited to becoming a fine character actor. He enjoyed trying out different outfits in his films, even appearing in drag one time as part of his love for experimentation. He just knew the right tone to employ to flesh out the character; here he was the hapless driver, the tough smuggler and the vulnerable father at the same time. Known for his penchant for innovative get-ups for his roles, he chose to model his looks on Abraham

Lincoln—the same beard, the frock coat and the bow.

Jeevan, another very dependable actor in Hindi cinema, brought his own comical brand of villainy to the screen. He was a Desai favourite, acting in many of his films. His personality fitted in perfectly with the light-hearted feel of the film; this was not a menacing villain but someone out of a comic book. You did not feel scared of him, but though you found him a bit ridiculous, you would not want to cross his path, since he was capable of murder.

The other two—Nirupa Roy and Mukri—were stalwarts too. Roy was the mother of choice in the 1970s, part martyr and part fighter, while Mukri was pitch perfect as the Muslim timber merchant with a glad eye who was also a strict father. Much is made of his lack of height; when Bachchan stands with his elbow on his head, or carries him into the hospital, it makes the audiences hoot with laughter.

Christian Lee Novetzke, associate professor of South Asian Studies at the University of Washington's Jackson School of International Studies, has studied *Amar Akbar Anthony* closely.

He feels Desai was certainly self-aware about what he was doing. 'Amar Akbar Anthony is certainly filled with clichés, and Desai's overt intention may have simply been, as so many directors do, to fill the film with all the things people want to see, and people often want to see clichés. But one thing that is distinctive about the film is exactly how and how many clichés it deploys. To this degree, don't you feel he is implying not an endorsement of them but an ironic vision of them?'

It is an intriguing argument, that Desai has his tongue firmly in his cheek when he twists clichés and presents them before his audience. It implies a bond between film-maker and filmgoer, an understanding that what is being shown is one big joke for entertainment value, not to be taken seriously. Certainly, Desai had a fear of being seen as a purveyor of messages or a maker of serious films, but it is debatable if he wanted to be just a creator of the ridiculous. There is much in Amar Akbar Anthony that is knowing and sly, but equally, the director is keen to tell a story and have that story taken seriously. The film is not a farce or a parody by any means.

Says Novetzke, 'It works because you are anticipating the ridiculous. When the outright nonsensical happens (moments when it seems Desai simply lost track of the story because scenes, of course, were not shot in a linear narrative way), it is subsumed under the general audacious romp that is the film.'

But Desai's go-go-go style and frenetic storytelling also had its faults. The illogicality of many sequences, intentional or otherwise, reduces what is otherwise a good film to a silly farce, which is a shame because Desai (and the actors) do take the film seriously and play it straight. Leave aside the 'miracle' scene when Nirupa Roy gets her eyesight back. That has to be taken with a pinch of salt, and it is.

However, there are many other plot twists, which get too much. The coincidences begin to pall after a while—every scene involving a cop leads directly to Inspector Amar, for example, which then brings him into contact with his brothers. The director contrives to bring the members of the Kishen Lal family face-to-face so many times that it gets tiresome. So much so that when other characters are introduced, it seems completely gratuitous and no one knows what to do with them. The actress Helen shows up in a scene when Kishen Lal greets her at the airport to fool Robert, who then kidnaps her thinking she is his daughter. Helen is kidnapped and brought to Robert's den where she promptly pulls out a gun, is disarmed and then taken away by Ranjeet, who plays Shabana Azmi's stepbrother. Nothing more is heard of her again. It all seems pointless.

There are several silly mistakes, some surely inadvertent. In one scene, Akbar addresses his doctor girlfriend Salma as Neetu, her real name. In the very next, she speaks about his 'Rh' blood group, which does not exist. All the brothers happily give blood that passes through one bottle into the mother. In the climax, Dr Salma feels Jenny's pulse and pronounces her pregnant. Were the villains stupid? They may well have been, since they completely miss the fact that the three men in front of them are singing the song 'Amar, Akbar, Anthony'. At least one of them, Anthony, is the man both Robert and Zebesco want to get their hands on.

All in good fun? Yes, but. There is no denying that the breeziness of the film keeps the viewer thoroughly entertained. And any viewer and lover of commercial Hindi cinema knows that along with all that masala, a large tablespoon of salt is very necessary to make the film consumable. Viewers are forgiving if the film-maker gives them a three-hour entertainment-filled package. *Amar Akbar Anthony* is most certainly entertaining. The ridiculous elements in it do not matter in the overall scheme of things. Desai was not fooling his audiences, he was inviting them in to laugh and cry along with him. No wonder he was rewarded with success. *Amar Akbar Anthony* was a stupendous hit and so were the films that followed, most of them conceived and executed in the same mould.

While some have argued that *Amar Akbar Anthony* was a film of its time and would not work today, Amitabh Bachchan differs. 'To those who say that it had too many miracles, coincidences and illogical twists, I can only point out the films of southern superstar Rajinikant which are huge successes today. You see a gun flying off his hand, shooting people and then coming back. Yet audiences are happy and convinced. It is a question of how the audience perceives the star and the film.' As far as *Amar Akbar Anthony* was concerned, there was certainly much suspension of disbelief, but the viewers felt engaged and entertained. They did not have to believe, they just had to sit back and enjoy.

5

The Manmohan Desai
School of Secularism

Secularism in India is quite different, in meaning and substance, from the secular idea elsewhere. It does not suggest, as is usually the case, the state's indifference to religion and religious practice. In India, the word implies respect for all religions. *Hindu, Muslim, Sikh, Isai, sabhi to hain bhai bhai* (Hindus, Muslims, Sikhs and Christians, all are brothers) is a good, popular way of expressing Indian secularism.

The Hindi film industry, which has a pan-Indian reach, strongly believes in this kind of secularism. It not only makes good business sense, but is also practical and sensible since the film industry itself is composed of people from all castes, creeds and religions. A film set is a microcosm of India itself, with people from diverse social and economic backgrounds working together as one. Over the decades, the industry has internalized this and film-makers have assiduously promoted harmony among different religious groups through cinema. Many early films, made in the pre-Independence era, actively propagated Hindu–Muslim unity, even as political parties were fighting on the basis of religion. The spectre of Partition gave a sense of urgency to film-makers such as V. Shantaram, whose 1941 film *Padosi* (also made in Marathi as *Shejari*) focused on the need for brotherhood between communities.

However, this secular attitude in our cinema comes with a rider. It is a common complaint among minorities that they are shown only as caricatures and stereotypes. In any typical Hindi commercial film, the main protagonists are usually Hindu, even if not always explicitly so. The leads have Hindu names that are caste-neutral though it is not difficult to conclude that they are from the upper castes. Religious minorities show up as supporting cast, and stereotypes abound. Muslims are usually kindly elders (the ubiquitous Rahim Chacha) or a supporting character (best friend, for example) who is given to uttering a few stock phrases in Urdu. Lately, Muslims have also been shown as menacing characters, such as a terrorist or an underworld don, but there is usually another 'good' Muslim character to compensate. Christians, a much tinier minority, have long complained that they get a raw deal—when they are not drunks or office secretaries, they are henchmen of the villains (Robert, Michael) or even vamps (Mona, Rita) and assorted cabaret dancers. There is the occasional clergyman, which inevitably leads to a church scene. Sikhs, one of the smallest groups, are represented as robustly brave or funny, with a penchant for breaking into a bhangra dance. And whenever there is a Parsi character, you can bet it will be someone hamming it up in their typical accent to evoke laughter. Things have begun to change in the face of protests from various community groups and a newer group of film-makers who are not given to older clichés, but many old habits persist.

The wounds of India's Partition were still very fresh around the time Manmohan Desai joined the film business. Many families were still separated, living in the two countries that had sprung up from one. In his very first film, *Chhalia*, Desai showed a willingness to try out something bold. Released in 1960, it touched upon the prejudices that were still very deeply embedded in people. The film was about a Hindu woman (played by Nutan) who had stayed back in Pakistan while her husband had moved to India. When she comes to him, he refuses to accept her and his small son, unsure of whose child it is. A small-time crook (Raj Kapoor) makes him see the error of his ways. Chhalia (trickster), as Raj Kapoor is called, is a happy-go-lucky man and sings, '*Hindu, Muslim, Sikh, Isai sabko mera salaam*' (I say hello to all).

Amar Akbar Anthony, though quite a different film, echoed a similar sentiment. There are several references to the unity of man and respect for all religions. This message is not hammered home and there is not a single dialogue extolling the virtues of such communal amity, but nor is there any subtlety in the way it is presented. The audience gets the message loud and clear, right from the moment the three brothers give blood to their mother, and three places of worship—a temple, a mosque and a church—can be seen from the windows behind them.

The film's title itself tells us a lot. The three names represent three religions, Hinduism, Islam, and Christianity. Professor Novetzke feels the film is about 'stereotypes of identity—each of the three brothers enters a stereotypical religious world. And so it is also about religious identity. But it can't be about actual identity—it totally eschews such complexity in a "social drama" sense. It strikes me that on one very basic level this is a film about the permissible possibilities for religious identity in secular India, or more specifically, in Hindu majoritarian (rather than Hindu chauvinistic) India. Each character's religious affiliation is carefully modulated to a Hindu secularist ideal.'

Film scholar Philip Lugdendorf in his blog post on the film has written: 'These are already signalled by the title's alliterative trinity of Sanskrit, Arabic, and English personal names, signalling (in properly descending demographic order) the Hindu, Muslim, and Christian communities whose essential unity and harmony—within the copious bosom of a (visibly Hindu) Mother India—is one of the film's (and Desai's personal favourite) themes.' The 'proper descending demographic order' may have had more to do with the rhythmic cadence of the title than any crafty plan, since in a later film *Naseeb*, the three names of the same waiter (Amitabh Bachchan) are John, Jaani, Janardan, exactly the opposite sequence.

The plot of *Amar Akbar Anthony* reflected Desai's interest in the idea of communal harmony, even in a kitschy, filmi way. It would have been easy to make all three lost sons 'Hindus', without overstressing the point. For example, they could have just been called Ajay, Vijay and Sanjay without harming the film's storyline. By making them belong to three different religions, Desai not only sent out his own powerful message, but also fully exploited the flavour each one offered. Interestingly, there is no overt 'Hinduness' in Amar's character, in the sense he does not pray or observe rituals, but the other two are obviously Muslim and Christian, and their clothes, accessories, accents, behaviour and lifestyle reflect that all the time.

Akbar, for example, is not only a Muslim, but

easily identified as such. While his foster-father, the man who picked him up from the park, is quite typically of the 'Rahim Chacha' variety, kind and devout, Akbar projects a different identity. He is street-smart, and is a qawwali singer, making him talented and, at a pinch, cultured. However, his is not high culture but a more popular one. He wears clothes that lower-middle-class boys from Muslim ghettos can (or could) be seen wearing—transparent shirts, netted vests and a skullcap. Clearly he is not particularly well off, since he lives in the ghetto and his foster-father continues his tailoring business. Akbar chews paan and it is suggested he too is quite religious, since he prays and sings devotional songs. It is possible that Akbar comes from a more Sufi tradition than from any specific Muslim denomination, as his qawwali to Saibaba's idol shows (which by itself was radical and somewhat controversial, since Islam prohibits idol worship). Some published references, chiefly Connie Haham's book on Manmohan Desai, have mentioned that there were objections to showing a Muslim praying to an idol. However, this could not be more than a stray opinion as no evidence has been found for this.

How different things were in the 1970s is also apparent from the fact that Akbar is a non-threatening character. The stereotyping of Muslims as somehow sinister came in much later; in this film, Akbar apologizes to Allah for what he is about to do—hit Robert during the fight scene in the end. This was done purposely, Rishi Kapoor pointed out, to emphasize Akbar's peaceful nature.

The other Muslim characters—Salma and Taiyyeb Ali—are fairly typical (by filmi standards), the former a doctor who wears a burqa when she goes out in public and the latter a timber merchant who is conservative when it comes to his daughters. Yet, the old man keeps a dancing girl as a mistress on the side.

As for Anthony, his Catholic identity is apparent to us right away. He goes to church regularly, prays and just in case anyone misses the point, wears a huge cross round his neck. The priest who found him outside the church years ago is like a father to him, who rebukes him about his ways but also loves him for his golden heart. Anthony has been trained well; he gives half his earnings to the church, cleans the premises and even goes for confessionals.

Like many other filmi Christians, Anthony uses a particular argot and runs a bar selling (illicit?) cheap liquor. Desai has said he had based Anthony on someone in his own neighbourhood who ran an illegal still. The lingo would be very familiar to Mumbai residents; there are thousands of such Anthonys around. Anthony also goes to dances at community clubs, again a common enough practice among young Mumbai Christians.

Jenny too is devout and at the same time social. But being a Christian (and having studied abroad), she is very liberal in the way she dresses. While Salma the Muslim is always in demure salwar-kameez and Lakshmi the Hindu switches to saris from bellbottoms the moment she discovers love and domesticity, Jenny wears dresses or skirts with slits running up to her thighs. These slits occasionally open, revealing a fair amount of skin. Desai ensures that it does not turn vulgar, but the filmi stereotyping of Christians as being more westernized (and therefore more 'liberated') allows him the liberty of infusing a bit of oomph to the character, and thus to the film.

Though the three brothers are brought up in three different religions by their respective foster-fathers, two of them (Akbar and Anthony) do not give it up once they know their true identity. Would their devout mother insist they change back to Hinduism? The film does not go into it of course, but it is worth conjecturing. The fact that all three have sweethearts from different religions suggests that religion would not be an issue in their 'real' family. Also, note that Kishen Lal brings up Jenny as a Christian because he knows that it is her original religion. He had kidnapped her from the bed of her father Robert, his enemy. Robert is a 'bad' Christian, who may profess to be respectful towards the fake priest Anthony but is a liar and a murderer, killing the real priest, and that too in a church. Kishen's liberal attitude towards Jenny's religion can be construed as doing the decent thing rather than bearing any overt message. Scriptwriter Anjum Rajabali says that forcing her to grow up as anything else would have appeared dishonourable, since it would amount to punishing a child for her father's crimes. (At one point, Rajabali points out, Jenny tells Kishen Lal, 'Bhagwan chahega to aapko apne bachche mil jayenge,' using Bhagwan instead of God. It probably was instinctive rather than intentional.)

Desai took care not to overemphasize religion, letting the plot speak for itself. This was a wise move, because it would have slowed down the film and brought in an extraneous element to it, diluting the fun. In an interview to Connie Haham, he is quoted as saying: 'Had I stood on a platform preaching "Hindu–Muslim bhai-bhai (brothers)", they would have said, "We don't want to hear that bullshit from you." So I said, best give it in a very palatable, say, homoeopathic pill. We gave a sugar-coated pill, they took it. They liked it. So we had communal harmony in it.' The message of unity and diversity is transmitted to the audience without sacrificing the entertainment aspect; heavy-handed moralizing or preaching would have made it boring and dull. In many a Hindi film, there is always a lecture at the end about how all religions are equal; Desai says that right up front in the title and leaves us to work it out.

The Indian nation was a different entity in the mid-1970s when *Amar Akbar Anthony* released. The cinema of the 1950s is often described as engaged in the nation-building process. The 1960s were about frothy confections, fun and joy, all in colour, with youngsters embracing their new-found freedom and going to the hills to romance and to picnic. The 1970s are often seen as the angry decade, a period full of frustration and despair, as a poor country dealt with internal and external shocks of inflation, political turmoil and the Emergency. This was the nation unsure of itself, with its foundations looking increasingly shaky and its most cherished notions being questioned. But *Amar Akbar Anthony* came at an interesting turning point. The Emergency was over and India had come out of a fiery test intact. The Indian nation was back on its feet. It is tempting to ask whether *Amar Akbar Anthony* was a reiteration of India's commitment to its nationhood, forcefully emphasizing secularism as a basic, unshakeable tenet.

Manmohan Desai would have been shocked to be told that he had indeed spread a message in *Amar Akbar Anthony*, since he made it a point to term himself a mere entertainer. And certainly the message is slipped in without any moralizing. In his later films he wasn't that nuanced—*Desh Premee* comes to mind—but in *Amar Akbar Anthony* he got the mix just right. Today, the phrase 'Amar Akbar Anthony' is used to signify communal amity and unity. It is a metaphor for multiculturalism of the most benign kind. Rajabali recalls a particularly piquant moment when the film was invoked: 'Soon after the carnage in Gujarat in 2002, some of us were discussing what we could do as artists to spread the message of communal harmony. And someone came up with the idea of turning *Amar Akbar Anthony* into a play and showing that we were all brothers, no matter what the religion. It didn't eventually happen, but I think it would have been a strong message indeed.' Could there be a greater tribute to Manmohan Desai and to the film?

6

Cosmopolitan Capers: The Mumbai Film

That *Amar Akbar Anthony* is a fairly typical 'masala' film of the 1970s with a secular bent is obvious and well established. What has not been analysed much is the fact that it is also a Mumbai film; not merely one made in Mumbai, the capital of India's Hindi film industry, but as one set in the city.

Mumbai has long been a location, a backdrop and even a character in Hindi films. Till the end of the 1940s, Hindi cinema was mainly preoccupied with historical and mythological themes, pulp action or social dramas. The big studios like Prabhat, New Theatres and Bombay

Talkies tended to specialize in one theme or the other. V. Shantaram's films were about social issues like communal discord or women's rights, while Sohrab Modi took the high road of historical narratives. New Theatres opted for literary adaptations. Urban cinema was conspicuously missing.

Gyan Mukherjee's big hit *Kismet* (1943) was among the first to be set in a city. By the end of that decade, a new crop of writers, directors and actors such as Raj Kapoor, K.A. Abbas, Chetan Anand, Shahid Latif and Dev Anand had emerged and their sensibilities were definitely urban, their outlook modern. They had moved to Mumbai and understood the angst and alienation of migrants. Their films therefore used the city in all its myriad shades as the background for their stories.

Neecha Nagar, Shri 420, Baazi, Taxi Driver— these were all films that spoke of how city dwellers at the bottom of the social rung managed to keep body, soul and integrity together as they negotiated the big bad urban world. The city was a dark and forbidding place, full of sharks and hustlers, but it was also a place of possibilities. You could be anonymous and casteless in a city and nobody would bother you unless you came in his way. Talent and skill, even (or especially) for illegal and sinful things, were always admired and in demand.

Since then, Mumbai has played its dutiful role in countless films of every genre. The city's cosmopolitanism, its frenetic buzz, its aloofness coupled with warmth, its glaring contrasts of extreme riches with frightening slums have all drawn film-makers of mainstream as well as art-house cinema. The city fascinates and repels at the same time, offering a director all the drama and emotion that he can possibly want.

The mid-1970s was also the period when the village, a staple of Hindi cinema for decades, all but disappeared from the screen. In the 1950s, the on-screen village was an innocent place, from where simple-minded people migrated due to economic reasons. Occasionally, the city invaded the idyllic rural environment and the encounter was inevitably tragic, at least for the villager. In *Barsaat*, Premnath comes to a lovely village, romances the naive belle (Nimmi) and then drives away in his swanky car, leaving her heartbroken. In *Tarana*, Dilip Kumar is a bit more honourable because he pines away for Madhubala even after he leaves her hamlet. And in *Do Bigha Zameen*, the poor farmer is exploited in the city (though one must note that he is also exploited in the village by the zamindar).

By the 1960s, the village was shot in full Technicolor and the damsels had rosy cheeks and healthy bodies, but they still fell for city slickers. Yet it was clear that India was gradually forgetting Mahatma Gandhi's message that 'real' India lived in its villages. Often, bucolic life was depicted as far from perfect—it was an environment where dacoits roamed with impunity and landlords assaulted women. It was abundantly clear that the attentions of directors were focused on the city, which was far more interesting and much more fun. It went without saying that the metropolis most in demand was Mumbai, which had so many stories to offer.

Desai was in love with Mumbai. His Mumbai was not the city of the rich, the glamorous or the powerful. He operated at the street level, where buses, cars and people jostled for space and where the ebb and flow of quotidian life were played out all the time. Growing up as he had in Khetwadi, one of the busiest and most cramped old neighbourhoods of the island part of the city, his ideal environment was noisy and bustling. People went about their business in a, well, business-like fashion, but the residents of a chawl, living almost on top of each other, made time for neighbours in their hour of need. The dense chawls of Mumbai, where he lived and had grown up, were a microcosm of the city itself, multilingual and multicultural, where privacy was non-existent. Everyone's joys and sorrows were shared, festivals were a large, communal affair and the evening was meant for gossip and catching up on the news.

In one of Desai's earliest films, *Bluff Master*, the hero (Shammi Kapoor) and his friends celebrate the festival of Janmashtami (the birth of Lord Krishna) just like it happens every year in various parts of Mumbai. Groups of young men get together and try and knock down an earthen pot with yogurt inside it; it commemorates the antics of the young Krishna who used to steal the butter his mother made. Tradition demands that spectators throw coloured water on the boys in a mock attempt to dissuade them. Desai would have surely grown up watching and maybe even participating in this annual spectacle.

Instead of shooting on the studio floors, which would have been easier, Desai chose to do it in Khetwadi. For this, he rounded up various young men and took the help of the local 'dadas' who would ensure things went smoothly. Shammi Kapoor, quite the big name of the time, sang and danced his way through the shoot. The song, 'Govinda aala re' has now become the unofficial anthem of the festival.

Many of his later films, however, were set in other locations and if at all they were shot in Mumbai, the city was incidental to the plot. But Amar Akbar Anthony is a resolutely Mumbai film and couldn't have been located anywhere else.

Imagine, for a moment, that the backdrop of the story shifted to Delhi. There would be many Amars in the city and an Akbar could conceivably be found in Chandni Chowk, which is a traditional Muslim neighbourhood. But Anthony, the church-going Catholic bootlegger? Never will Delhi produce such a character. He belongs to the many Christian enclaves of Mumbai, such as Vasai, Byculla or Bandra. No, it had to be Mumbai, because more than just the protagonists themselves, the underlying cosmopolitan idea behind Amar

Akbar Anthony belonged here. Their individual lives and their interconnectedness would not be possible elsewhere.

So Anthony was located in the western suburb of Bandra, a fact that is made known to the audience halfway in the film. Viewers from the city would also have recognized Mount Mary church, a beautiful structure on a hill in the west. Anthony wears wide-bottom flares, as was the fashion of the day, and instead of a shirt prefers colourful leather jackets. Both his home and his bar (licence number 102), however, are ramshackle, to say the least, as would be most 'country' liquor bars in the city. These dens serve liquor at cheap prices to their working-class customers and appeared in many a Hindi film right from the 1950s. The area where he lives is called Anthonywadi and it is suggested that he has muscled in while the earlier local boss was away in jail. These small touches lend an air of authenticity. Some Mumbaikars may carp at the obvious error of the young middle son running from a park in Borivali to take shelter at a Bandra church, since the two suburbs are quite distant from each other, but that is a small quibble.

The set design for Akbar's neighbourhood is also authentic. The passers-by, the low-rise structures, the timber warehouses, all paint a picture of a Muslim ghetto of the type that dotted Mumbai in the 1970s. Desai and his team knew their city and had taken pains to replicate it as realistically as they could.

The dialogues too are as close to the real lingo as possible. Kader Khan says he used to imagine each character speaking and then write it down. When Anthony says to Akbar in an early scene of the film, '*Tum aajkal diktaich nahin hai*', it is wrong Hindi, but accurate Mumbai street language.

Hindi films do not have spoken lines; they have 'dialogues' and these tend to be epigrammatic, elliptical, flowery, bombastic and heavily laden with symbolism. Actors tend to declaim and many a career has been built upon the skill of an actor in speaking the colourful dialogues written for him. Both writers and actors often aim to please the frontbenchers with florid speech, and in films with two big actors, one is constantly trying to trip up the other.

Kader Khan, no slouch himself at theatrical

writing, naturally outdid himself in *Amar Akbar Anthony*. With so much scope for drama and high emotion, he had plenty of opportunities to write some strong lines. But he was also aware that this was a film in which the main characters were all ordinary Joes, most of them perhaps with limited education. Hence, he curbed his natural flair and stuck to everyday speech, which is what gives *Amar Akbar Anthony* its flavour. Anthony's witticisms—for example, when he explains to the priest that the ideal girl for him is someone who can make violins play in the background—sound plausible, since that is just the kind of talk that would come from a young boy.

Manmohan Desai and Kader Khan both had Mumbai deeply embedded in their souls. Khetwadi and Kamathipura, where they grew up, are not far from each other as the crow flies. But they are worlds apart in terms of their character. Khetwadi is resolutely middle-class and bourgeois, notwithstanding its tenement buildings, while Kamathipura is home to Mumbai's biggest red-light area. Kader Khan says his family kept him away from all the muck around them— prostitution, gambling dens, illicit liquor bars—

but it was difficult to totally escape all that. 'One street had prostitutes, the other eunuch gangs and the third liquor and gambling dens. I used to study in my room from where I could watch the prostitutes doing their business across the street.' The young Kader buried his head in the classics—Gorky, Chekhov and Manto—but a lot of Kamathipura and its colourful atmosphere must have got into his system. He got the language of the street just right in the film.

Ironically, this kind of language has become normal in Hindi films, where the hero uses it regardless of whether it suits the role or not. Bazaar language is now supposed to be cool and with-it, and actors love to use it because it gives them cred and works with the punters. Where the emphasis used to be on long-winded, ornate lines, it has now gone to the other extreme of the pendulum and become 'tapori' (vagabond). Kader Khan blames himself for this, saying it was his lines for Anthony that are responsible for this trend. 'Now I must do something to redeem myself and reverse this trend,' he says.

Kader Khan loved the character of Akbar the most even if Anthony got all the laughs. 'My favourite is Akbar—subtle and nuanced. But Bachchan was a star, so his role got the most publicity.' Rishi Kapoor, who had a meaty role and sang no less than five songs, also notes the emphasis on Amitabh Bachchan. 'He was so big at the time. But I stood my ground in *Amar Akbar Anthony* and in the other films I worked with him, *Kabhi Kabhie*, *Coolie* and *Naseeb*.'

Mumbai is not mentioned in the film even once, though there are fleeting references to places like Borivali and Bandra. The old home of Kishen Lal and his family is in a part of Bandra and Anthony lives in the same suburb, which is traditionally seen as a Catholic-dominated one. The film was shot in various locations in and around Mumbai and some of these are quite recognizable. Much of it was filmed on indoor sets in studios such as Ranjit, RK and Kamalistan, but many crucial scenes, like the qawwali for Saibaba, were shot on what was then the outskirts of the city. 'The area in Borivali, where we built the set for the Saibaba temple, was a jungle; today it is a concrete jungle, full of buildings,' recalls Ketan Desai, giving voice to the oft-heard plaint of the Mumbai resident. The Bachchan portion of the song '*Humko tumse ho gaya hai pyaar*' was filmed on the quiet Aksa beach. For indoor church scenes they chose Don Bosco, while the more impressive facade of Mount Mary church in Bandra was used for the outdoor shots.

The film exudes 1970s' Mumbai cool, though we now look back at it as kitsch. Bachchan wears wide flares and a leather jacket and sports his signature hairstyle. Vinod Khanna's haircut would not pass muster with the police department, but then he is a film star and is thus excused. His trousers too are ever so tapered and his uniform is cut to show off his streamlined physique. When he takes off his shirt to fight Anthony, he is wearing a sleeveless vest, rather than being bare-chested, establishing his somewhat conservative persona. He is after all the elder brother and a cop and thus cannot be radical in his sartorial choices. Rishi Kapoor as Akbar comes across as a cool boy from a Muslim ghetto; his outfit of choice—the transparent shirt, the netted vest—are all clichéd, in the manner of many Muslim young men—but adequately convey that he is with-it, at least within his own environment.

The women too wore the latest fashions: Neetu

Singh, as Salma, is conservatively dressed as good Muslim girls are, but sports her trademark big hoop earrings; Shabana Azmi is seen in smart flares as long as she is a working girl who cheats innocent men, but switches to cotton saris the moment she moves into the respectable confines of Amar's home. Parveen Babi's foreign-returned Jenny flaunts colourful dresses, glorious, wide-brimmed hats and the occasional skirt with a long slit that shows her legs.

The overall impact is one of style, because without it, a mainstream commercial film would end up looking cheap and tacky, or worse, like a realistic art film. Commercial film-makers spend a lot of money on production values, realizing that audiences come to see well-dressed stars as much as to hear the songs or enjoy the dances.

A lot of attention is also paid to the costumes. In Mumbai's Hindi films, stars often come with their own preferred designers and the producer and director go along with it. Bachchan's clothes were always designed by Kachin, one of the bigger names of the era; it didn't matter what the theme of the film was or what the character demanded. The important thing was to make the star look good, not necessarily authentic.

One of the designers was Leena Daru, who by then had about a decade's experience in Mumbai films. A graduate in fine arts from JJ School of Art, Mumbai, she was the preferred designer for many heroines, including Neetu Singh who wore her creations in several films. 'Manmohanji said I leave it to you—money is no issue. Neetu's character was a Muslim, so I gave her salwar-kameezes and shararas, but stylish ones. Parveen Babi liked what I had done for Neetu and asked me to design her skirts and dresses too. Most of what she wears in the film was done by me.'

All this made *Amar Akbar Anthony* a very contemporary film. But is it a modern film? It certainly looks it. The clothes reflect current fashion, the sets are smartly designed, the references are *au courant* (gold smuggling, for example.)

But its social attitudes send out mixed signals. The youngsters are modern enough, and are in control of their lives. There seem to be no parental restrictions, which was not necessarily the case in India of the time. Both the men and women are free to follow their own interests, except perhaps in the case of Salma, whose father is extremely conservative. This is in keeping with the general perception of Muslims who are seen as traditional and even orthodox and certainly do not allow 'freedom' to their daughters. Yet, she is a doctor, an interesting choice of profession, and clearly has interaction with males. And her father accepts he has made a mistake in keeping her apart from Akbar because he can see that the boyfriend is a decent sort. When the Kishen Lal family unites at the end of the film, the women do not fall at the feet of the parents, a common enough scene in Hindi films of the time. Desai was not a social conservative by any means.

However, the constant references to religion, prayer, belief, and even superstition reflect an unease with modernity. Religion plays an important role in the lives of Anthony and Akbar, since they are adopted and presumably given a religious upbringing. This could be to emphasize their religious identity, a story device more than anything else. Amar is never shown praying— perhaps as a Hindu he does not have to necessarily go to a temple or even have a shrine at home. But his mother more than makes up for it; she is the custodian of the family's traditions and wears the Santoshi Maa locket. (Santoshi Maa had become

big after a film about her became an unlikely hit
in 1975. Inserting her into *Amar Akbar Anthony*
was no doubt an attempt to introduce one more
spice into the meal.) The father—Kishen Lal—
wears the locket but only out of sentiment.

The characters all look urban, but the mother
could well be from a more conservative, small-
town background. She wears her sari in a very
old-fashioned style and though she does not age
over twenty-two years, she looks old to begin
with. Also, since she has no one to look after her
and probably just gets by with help from friends
and neighbours, she has no other clothes. And she
exudes the requisite amount of helplessness. In
fact, for all Desai's claimed emphasis on the
mother figure, Nirupa Roy in *Amar Akbar Anthony*
remains a sketchy character, put there only to
prop up the men. She has not one worthy scene
to herself and is a Calamity Jane, getting into
scrapes and accidents all the time. This is
intriguing, as Roy had played a tough mother in
Deewaar, where she had no hesitation in pointing
out the error of his ways to Vijay, played by
Amitabh Bachchan. Here she is reduced to a mere
figurehead, a prop used to set up various scenes.

The father on the other hand is a powerful character, not in his relationship with his sons but as a canny driver-turned-smuggler who outwits his rival at every step.

And it goes without saying that each of the men chooses a girl from his own community—it would probably be too much to expect a mainstream entertainer of the 1970s to complicate matters on that score.

7

The Last Word in Entertainment

With *Amar Akbar Anthony*, Manmohan Desai, already one of the more commercially successful directors in the Mumbai film industry, became a superstar among film-makers. All the four films that he had been making simultaneously turned out to be box-office hits. But it was *Amar Akbar Anthony* that consolidated his position as the man with the Midas touch, his finger firmly on the pulse of the 'janata', i.e., the masses.

When the film was released, the critics were unsparing in their ridicule, though they acknowledged that the film had its moments.

'Outright hokum is what the film is, but redeemed by the hilarity that accompanies it,' wrote Bikram Singh, the influential reviewer of the *Times of India*. He praised a couple of scenes, including the climax and the mirror sequence, but felt that Desai had been inspired by American musicals, whose influence was visible in the song *'My name is Anthony Gonsalves'*. The headline of the review said it all: 'Absurd yet funny'.

'Manmohan has blended it with the right dose of emotion, sentiments, fights, romance, songs, comedy and what not, and he has not left out anything, all wrapped up in flamboyance and opulence,' said the weekly *Blitz*. 'The whole thing may sound incredible but in between, and taken with a pinch of salt, it provides fascinating fare.' Bachchan's turn as the drunk was called 'sheer delight' and the newspaper noted that the girls were just there for cosmetic value, a point made by several other reviewers.

Nor were readers impressed. The film magazine *Filmfare* in its edition dated 5 August 1977 carried letters from irate readers who sneered at the 'miracle' of the mother getting back her eyesight, saying that eye operations would not be needed any more. Another complained that viewers were being forced to accept 'such absurdity as entertainment'.

Desai was, however, unperturbed. A few carping souls aside, audiences had loved the film and that was enough for him. He also decided that he would henceforth make films only for himself rather than for other production companies. *Suhaag*, his next release, was produced by Sharma Cine Associates—possibly a long-standing commitment—but after that every film he directed was for the home company.

He was also convinced that many of his tricks and devices, the lost-and-found formula being the most obvious one, were sure-fire winners and saw no reason to jettison them. There were many other 'Manmohanisms' that had become his stock-in-trade, such as unity among different religious and ethnic groups, the suffering mother, and the bullying by power structures that oppressed the masses. These were staples present in most of his films after *Amar Akbar Anthony*. Above all, he had his trump card, Amitabh Bachchan. Desai once said that a star like Bachchan came 'only once in 76 years' and now that he had established a rapport with him, he was not about to let go. So far, the two had worked only in *Parvarish* and *Amar Akbar Anthony*; with the latter's stupendous success, they became a team.

Bachchan's other favourite director of the period was Prakash Mehra, who directed his first bona fide commercial success *Zanjeer,* and they were a comfortable unit too. There was a third director too, Yash Chopra, who worked with Bachchan on five films, two of them being among his best, *Deewaar* and *Kabhi Kabhie.* Interestingly, Bachchan made the most number of films with Hrishikesh Mukherjee, the high priest of what came to be known as 'middle-class cinema', with clean storylines that would appeal to family audiences; but this association is often overlooked. As far as Bachchan's films of the period are concerned, it is the Desai–Mehra rivalry that is spoken of the most.

Where Mehra had created, with the help of Salim-Javed's sizzling script, the Angry Young Man at war with the establishment, a stereotype that has stuck with Bachchan till this day, Desai completely discarded it by giving Bachchan a completely new filmi avatar. Interestingly, Mehra had made *Hera Pheri* in 1976 in which Bachchan and Vinod Khanna played funny con men, but not till *Amar Akbar Anthony* did Bachchan's image undergo a paradigm shift. Bachchan insists that this transition was not a deliberate move on his part, just as he has always maintained that he did not work on getting the Angry Young Man's roles, they just happened. But something did change. In Desai's films, Bachchan was angry, happy, jolly, frivolous, romantic and happy-go-lucky, all at the same time. He became both the hero and the comedian. It can be safely said that the Bachchan of Desai's films almost single-handedly felled the on-screen comedian since there was no need to hire someone else to do what he did so well. It was a leap of imagination on Desai's part to risk discarding a well-entrenched persona and create an entirely new and radically different one. It became the template of Bachchan films for many years to come and was successfully adopted by other actors as well. It is not uncommon today to see leading actors acting the fool on the screen, something that in an earlier era would have been left to the comedian.

After *Suhaag*—another lost-and-found formula

movie—Desai made *Naseeb*, which in many ways is *Amar Akbar Anthony* lite, with Bachchan playing a waiter with the unlikely name of John Jaani Janardan, signifying all three major religions. Perfidiousness, coincidences and reconciliation, all the familiar themes from *Amar Akbar Anthony* were present. The climax of *Naseeb* had an uncanny similarity to the final scenes of *Amar Akbar Anthony*—here too the three heroes (accompanied by their loved ones) storm the villain's lavish den, a revolving restaurant atop a skyscraper, wearing outlandish disguises: a matador (Bachchan), a Cossack (Shatrughan Sinha) and Charlie Chaplin (Rishi Kapoor) accompanied, of all people, by a Spanish flamenco dancer (Hema Malini), a harem girl (Reena Roy) and Eliza Doolittle (Kim) in the famous dress she wore at the races. Don't look for meaning or logic here. The villains naturally are fooled by these clever costumes, just like in *Amar Akbar Anthony*. The audience is complicit in this and goes along, enjoying the song, knowing fully well how it will all end.

The film was a big success, though it has a jaded and frayed look today, unlike *Amar Akbar Anthony* which still retains its polish and freshness.

The Desai–Bachchan juggernaut continued to roll along with *Desh Premee* (national integration), *Coolie* (lost-and-found, working class versus the criminal rich and dollops of Islamic culture) and *Mard* (Indians versus cruel British rulers and their Indian compradors). All the films had the 'Manmohan Desai touch', which by now had begun to translate as Manmohan Desai clichés. In *Coolie*, the mother, played by Waheeda Rehman, gets her speech back when she sees her son after many years, a la Nirupa Roy who regains her eyesight in *Amar Akbar Anthony*. There were animals galore, performing stunts and proving to be faithful friends (a hawk in *Coolie* and a horse and a dog in *Mard*). There were comedic set pieces. In *Coolie*, Bachchan pretends to be a statue (in a garden suspiciously like the one used in *Amar Akbar Anthony*) or goes into impossible contortions as Rati Agnihotri keeps switching the radio channels between a yoga programme and a cookery show about making an omelette. In *Mard*, you have a drunk Bachchan playing to the gallery sitting on a statue of a horse, or you have another version of the mirror scene, this time with Prem Chopra filling in for his reflection.

It was all vintage Manmohan Desai, outlandish, creative and funny, but also, surprisingly, crude—which no one can accuse *Amar Akbar Anthony* of being. Desai, who prided himself on being a film-maker for families and kept his movies clean—*Amar Akbar Anthony* is devoid of anything that could embarrass anyone—began sneaking in crass scenes into his films. *Mard*, in particular, is an embarrassment, with double entendres and sexist attitudes galore, which leave one cringing. The song '*Hum to tambu mein*' (referring to implanting a bamboo stick in a tent), for example, leaves no doubt in the listeners' mind about what is going on.

Coolie is perhaps the best film Desai made after *Amar Akbar Anthony*. It has some genuinely touching, warm and funny moments and Bachchan is convincing as a porter on a railway platform. After a long time he essayed a role that was rooted in real life, playing a character many people from the working classes (the bulk of cinema-goers) could identify with. (Of course, one can argue: where in the world do you get a coolie who forcibly carries off the boss's daughter, or who barges into his employer's palatial mansion and ransacks it, or who brings the railway station to a standstill with a call for hartal? The answer is self-evident: in a Manmohan Desai film.) That he was Muslim added a certain extra dimension to the role, since this was a rarity on the Indian screen. In the Hindi film business, it helps to have a hero who is of indeterminate caste and linguistic affiliation, but everyone must know he is a Hindu. Making the biggest star of the day a Muslim (and not turning it into a Muslim social) was a brave but also smart idea, since it reached out to the large Muslim audience. Desai had often said that he was fascinated by Islamic culture, but the box-office implications couldn't have been lost on him. Interestingly, the girl whom the coolie loves is Julie D'Costa, a Christian; making her a Hindu could perhaps have been needlessly provocative. But then, Sunny, a Hindu orphan is brought up as a son by Salma, Iqbal Khan's mother, so it all balances out in the Manmohan Desai universe.

Desai's golden touch was, however, intact and both *Coolie* and *Mard* were hits—in the case of *Coolie*, helped no doubt by the infamous accident that almost took Bachchan's life.

In 1984, after the assassination of Prime Minister

Indira Gandhi, her son Rajiv Gandhi appealed to his childhood friend Amitabh Bachchan to join him in active politics. Bachchan, on top of his game at the time, with an almost uninterrupted run at the top for twelve years, agreed and won a handsome victory from Allahabad, his home town. This made him a member of Parliament, which automatically meant less time for the movie business.

In the whole of 1985, Bachchan shot for just one film, *Aakhree Raasta*, which released the year after. His last big film *Mard* had been released in 1985. Bachchan resigned from his parliamentary post halfway in his five-year tenure and went back to the shooting floor with his friend Manmohan Desai. But the world had changed in the brief interim. A new crop of young actors had emerged, audience tastes had changed and Desai seemed to have lost his mojo and storytelling skills. The film they chose to work on was called *Ganga Jamuna Saraswati*, an unbelievably tired effort all round, which lacked both logic and conviction. Desai tried out every trick in the book and then some, including casting Mithun Chakraborty—the pretender to Bachchan's top slot at the time—as

Bachchan's friend, but the final product was a hotchpotch that just did not make any sense. Not that Manmohan Desai's films needed to make sense or were expected to, but this one failed to entertain—a cardinal error if you want your audience to leave their brains behind.

Kader Khan, who had stuck on with Desai, recalls telling the latter that he had to guard against becoming too outlandish. 'I don't think he liked it when I told him that he couldn't just put in anything. And when he included a scene in *Ganga Jamuna Saraswati* showing Bachchan carrying a crocodile, I knew it was time to move on.' He left and another dialogue writer was brought in.

The film was conceived as some sort of sequel to *Amar Akbar Anthony*. Some have speculated that it was even titled *Amar Akbar Anthony 2* during the pre-shoot period, and two other stars, Jeetendra and the ever-reliable Rishi Kapoor, were signed up but not included. In the end the only other male co-star was Mithun Chakraborty.

Ganga Jamuna Saraswati flopped resoundingly. It must have been a blow for the man who had continuously directed hits. Smart man that he was, he would have realized that the connection he had with his audiences had broken. Perhaps it was time for a newer, younger generation to take over.

For his next, *Toofan*, he handed over the reins to his son Ketan who was by then a fully trained director, having worked with his father for over a decade. He roped in Salim Khan (of Salim-Javed fame) as the story, screenplay and dialogue writer. Salim and Javed had just split up after an enviable run of almost twenty films and had gone their own way. And he gave Ketan not one but two Amitabh Bachchans, in the shape of a double role, with one playing a magician and the other Toofan, a heroic figure, part Robin Hood and part Zorro. Surely this would please the audiences!

It did not. *Toofan* too dived at the box office, proving that every star, every producer and every idea has a sell-by date. The separated-at-birth theme was now officially dead. (There haven't been many films since then and now the whole idea looks quaint and outdated, retro at best.)

Interestingly, in the same year (1989), Bachchan also played a magician in *Jaadugar*. This time the director was Prakash Mehra. This movie too was a resounding disaster. The star's long and successful tenure with both Desai and Mehra came to an end with flops.

Desai, despondent and perhaps lacking motivation, did not make any film after that and died in 1994. On 1 March that year, he allegedly committed suicide, jumping off his building in Khetwadi, where he had moved back after living for a few years in a tony neighbourhood. He was said to be suffering from chronic back pain.

But he has left behind an important filmic legacy. He was the biggest director of the 1970s and his films set new benchmarks for entertainment and racy storytelling, to say nothing about commercial success. Though not all his films are of consistently high quality, many of them deserve to be studied and certainly *Amar Akbar Anthony* will always be an iconic film, not the least because it is the benchmark 1970s entertainer. It is a movie that has travelled well and, even three-and-a-half decades later, is still a delight to watch.

Desai's peers often praised his work, though there was always implicit criticism in their remarks. In Connie Haham's book, Shyam Benegal is quoted as saying: 'I respect Manmohan Desai for his honesty, for never having claimed to be anything but an entertainer. I think Manmohan Desai is totally uninterested in social messages; everything happens by miracle on screen. People leave the cinema without taking any messages, but they have been entertained.'

This assertion is open to challenge. Throughout his career, especially in the latter half, Desai did have something to say in his films. His films promoted the notion of unity in diversity, of the importance of family and the triumph of good over evil. His technique was not artsy, perhaps not even subtle, but it got the point across without hammering it home. No one could have left the cinema without the emotional satisfaction of knowing that a kind of equilibrium had been restored and the bad guys had got what was coming to them.

The secular message was conveyed even more strongly. *Amar Akbar Anthony* more than once tells us that in India all religious groups are equal, brothers under the skin. Structural analysts may look for deeper meanings in the way this idea has been put across but can anyone dispute its existence? That Kishen Lal brings up Jenny, whom he had kidnapped as a baby from Robert, as a Christian and who then falls in love with Anthony (who is not a Christian by birth) is a powerful point. The same applies to the Akbar–Salma pairing. The mother, Bharti, is a devout and orthodox Hindu woman but we have to presume that she accepts all three of her daughters-in-law; there is no evidence to suggest otherwise. The qawwali to an idol of Shirdi Saibaba by the Muslim Akbar too is symbolic of the mystic's following among devotees of all religious groups. (Desai himself became a regular visitor to Shirdi after his wife died in 1979, since she was a great follower of the saint.)

The Mumbai film-maker has his own signals and codes which he uses to send messages out to the audience, and the latter have, over the years, developed skills and resources to pick them up. In another era, most notably in the 1940s, when India was ruled by the British and censorship laws were stringent, directors often inserted allegorical references to rebellion against the invader; the censors let those scenes through and there was little doubt among the masses what the message was. Since then, unity in diversity, equal respect for all faiths and regions, and the fundamentally secular nature of the country have been staple themes of Hindi cinema, often dished out amid dollops of entertainment. While some films preach, others prefer to let the story do the talking. Desai was among the latter, even if his style was not as nuanced as that of the art-house directors. His deployment of crude miracles to get a point across would definitely offend a more refined sensibility, but his heart was in the right place.

Many versions of the film were made, including a Telugu one (*Ram Rahim*) and one in Malayalam (*John Jaffer Janardhan*). Both had top stars, including Rajinikant and Mammootty. Both were huge successes. An interesting twist to the tale is that in 1978, a Pakistani film (in Punjabi) called *Akbar, Amar, Anthony* was released. Amar, in this version, was a Sikh. The story centred around a family which breaks up during Partition. The sons grow up with foster-families as a Muslim, a Sikh and a Christian. At the end of the film they are all united and the grown-up boys convert to Islam. The film flopped.

Of late, there has been talk of remaking *Amar Akbar Anthony*. An imagination-bereft industry has been looking at the past for inspiration; *Amar Akbar Anthony* is an obvious choice. Kitsch, 1970s style, is in, as witnessed in the success of films like *Om Shanti Om*. David Dhawan—director of many comedies in the 1990s, and someone whose collaborations with Govinda in the decade had the film press comparing the duo to the Manmohan Desai–Amitabh partnership—declared he would take a shot at it and even approached some of the old technicians of Desai's films to help him out. Nothing has come of it yet, but occasionally the film press carries articles about its revival. It will be a major vanity project for any actor.

Can it be remade? No reason why it cannot; yet there are several ifs and buts. To begin with, three big heroes and three equally top female actors will have to be convinced to come on board, which is not an easy thing. Moreover, the world has changed since the 1970s and with it, filmgoers too. Indian audiences expect different things today and may not swallow the miracles that Desai dished out so glibly. They are more exposed to global trends, and their sensibilities, at least in the cities, are in tune with their counterparts in other parts of the world. Their entertainment needs are met through a variety of sources, from television to the Internet to even mobile phones. They consume entertainment differently. *Amar Akbar Anthony* is an entertainer, but more as a curiosity piece, a relic of an era long gone. There is nostalgia, yes, but there is no saying if nostalgia will translate into success for a remake.

Yet the point must be made that many younger film directors today could learn a thing or two from Manmohan Desai's school of film-making and most of all, from *Amar Akbar Anthony*. His clear delineation of characters, his firm grip on the art of good storytelling and his commitment to his viewing public are all skills and values that are in short supply. His heart and spirit were with the man in the front benches who had spent his hard-earned money to sit in that darkened hall for three hours and wanted to be entertained; there is not a trace of self-consciousness in Desai's art. He never shot a film abroad, had no need for exotic locations and did not bother with placing large numbers of pelvis-thrusting women in the background; for him, it was all about the story.

That is why we still remember him and still

enjoy a few laughs and shed a tear or two when we watch *Amar Akbar Anthony* all these years later. Surely, the final words belong to Amitabh Bachchan, Desai's favourite star: 'I love all my films and roles equally. But just the other day, I was cruising channels on television and came across *Amar Akbar Anthony*—it was the climax scene. And I stopped to watch it for some time. I rarely ever do that.'

Principal Cast and Crew

CAST

Vinod Khanna: Inspector Amar Khanna
Rishi Kapoor: Akbar Ilhabadi
Amitabh Bachchan: Anthony Gonsalves
Neetu Singh: Dr Salma Ali
Parveen Babi: Jenny
Shabana Azmi: Lakshmi
Nirupa Roy: Bharati
Pran: Kishen Lal
Jeevan: Robert
Yusuf Khan: Zebesco
Mukri: Taiyyab Ali
Nasir Hussain: Catholic Priest
Kamal Kapoor: Superintendant Khanna
Hercules: Raghu

CREW

Produced by: Manmohan Desai and Subhash Desai
Directed by: Manmohan Desai
Screenplay: Prayag Raaj
Dialogue: Kader Khan
Music: Laxmikant-Pyarelal
Lyrics: Anand Bakshi
Cinematography: Peter Pereira
Editing: Kamlakar Karkhanis
Art direction: A. Rangaraj
Sound re-recordist: Mangesh Desai
Audiographer: Kuldeep Singh
Associate re-recordist: Kuldip Sood
Special effects: Kirit Kumar
Titles designer: G.D. Art
Special effects: Ramesh Meer and Peter Pereira
Stunts: Ravi Khanna

Acknowledgements

A whole book on just one film? Exploring all aspects of a film in detail is a tempting thought, but not an easy project, as soon became evident when I set out to tackle *Amar Akbar Anthony*. It is one of those iconic films that everyone in India—from the serious film buff to the curious, occasional filmgoer—has seen. Those who missed it the first time round, when it was just released, would have caught it during its innumerable reruns on television. It is the kind of film people remember fondly, and whose very mention brings a knowing smile to their faces. Could anything new be said about it?

It turned out that there was much that was waiting to be discovered. The making of the film was full of interesting stories and anecdotes, and the movie itself was open to several analyses and interpretations.

But such an undertaking required help—from those who had been involved in its making, on camera as well as behind the scenes. The man who brought it all together is unfortunately no more with us. Manmohan Desai had conceived and controlled this madcap film from beginning to end. It was his vision, which he held on to in the face of scepticism—of the stars and several others around him. Fortunately, there was an excellent book on him, and the author, Connie Haham, very generously allowed me to quote from it.

Ketan Desai, the director's son, was a young assistant on the sets of *Amar Akbar Anthony*, and happily recalled anecdotes about his father and his style of functioning. The stars of the film were all forthcoming because they had had such a good time making it. Amitabh Bachchan, of course, is a model interviewee, coming up with tiny details that add much value to any story. Rishi Kapoor promptly agreed to meet, and then recounted stories about Manmohan Desai and his offbeat ideas. Shabana Azmi, music director Pyarelal and even the reclusive Kader Khan gladly recalled their experiences while working on the film. Ramesh Meer recounted how the 'miracles'— which are an integral part of *Amar Akbar Anthony*—were created. The retired cameraman Peter Pereira, puzzled why anyone should track him down to talk about something he had done years ago, was voluble as he went down memory lane. Nasreen Munni Kabir opened up her phone book to provide me with contacts. I wish to thank all of them for their generosity.

A special thanks to the team at HarperCollins, particularly V.K. Karthika and editor Shantanu Ray Chaudhuri. Shantanu brings enormous knowledge of Hindi cinema and ensures that writers are kept on the straight and narrow, especially when it comes to facts.

I have to, of course, acknowledge the enormous patience of my wife Almona who, despite her puzzlement at my wanting to see the film over and over again, did not mind. Though it did help that she liked *Amar Akbar Anthony* as much as I did.